Oriens

ORIENS

A Pilgrimage Through Advent and Christmas

November 27, 2022 – February 2, 2023

FR. JOEL SEMBER

Our Sunday Visitor
Huntington, Indiana

Nihil Obstat
Msgr. Michael Heintz, Ph.D.
Censor Librorum

Imprimatur
✠ Kevin C. Rhoades
Bishop of Fort Wayne-South Bend
February 23, 2022

The *Nihil Obstat* and *Imprimatur* are official declarations that a book is free from doctrinal or moral error. It is not implied that those who have granted the *Nihil Obstat* and *Imprimatur* agree with the contents, opinions, or statements expressed.

Our Sunday Visitor Publishing Division, Our Sunday Visitor, Inc., 200 Noll Plaza, Huntington, IN 46750; www.osv.com; 1-800-348-2440

ISBN: 978-1-68192-781-7 (Inventory No. T2737)
1. RELIGION—Holidays—Christmas & Advent.
2. RELIGION—Christian Living—Prayer.
3. RELIGION—Christianity—Catholic.

eISBN: 978-1-68192-782-4
LCCN: 2022936090

Cover design: Tyler Ottinger / Melissa Schlegel
Cover art: Lisa Dorschner
Interior design: Amanda Falk

PRINTED IN THE UNITED STATES OF AMERICA

Dedicated to Saint Athanasius,
Bishop and Doctor of the Church

+

and to the parish families of
Saint John the Evangelist,
Ss. Mary & Hyacinth,
Saint Wenceslaus, and
Ss. James & Stanislaus
Thank You

+

¡Buen Camino!

Presentation of the Lord

Week 10

Week 9

Week 8

Baptism of the Lord

Epiphany (Observed)   Week 7

Epiphany of Our Lord

Mary the Mother of God

Holy Family   Week 6

Christmas Octave Days

Nativity of Our Lord   Week 5

Christmas countdown begins   Week 4

St. Lucy

Our Lady of Guadalupe   Week 3

Immaculate Conception

St. Nicholas

Week 2

St. Andrew

Week 1

Contents

Introduction

Give a man a fish, and you feed him for a day.
Teach a man to pray, and you feed him for a lifetime.

TEACH A MAN TO PRAY ...

There are many wonderful Advent books full of moving meditations for you to choose from. This isn't one of them. Instead of giving you my meditations, this book will teach you how to meditate for yourself. If you don't really know how to pray with Scripture, this book will teach you. If you already know how to pray, then it will help you to pray better. I left space each day for you to journal your prayer experiences. When you get to the end of the book, you will find that it has become full of moving meditations, but they won't be my meditations; they'll be yours. I hope that, as you learn to go deeper in your conversations with God, prayer becomes your favorite part of each day, and this season takes on a whole new meaning.

IF YOU PRAYED WITH *ORIENS* BEFORE

You might be wondering how this book compares with previous editions. The format is exactly the same: We teach *lectio divina* and imaginative prayer, provide a Scripture passage each day, and give you space to journal. You will encounter familiar figures like John the Baptist, Zechariah, and, of course, Mary and Joseph. Most of the Scripture passages are completely new in order to match with Lectionary Cycle A. New themes appear and new faces like Noah and the prodigal son. Only fourteen Scripture passages will be familiar to you, primarily in the countdown to Christmas and a few feast days like the Holy Innocents. *Oriens* 2022 will be like walking down a familiar road, but with new companions and at a new place in your life. If you've never done *Oriens* before, finish reading the Introduction and then skim the rest of the introductory material through the first day (Sunday, November 27). That will give you a good sense of the road ahead.

"DO YOU WANT TO WALK *THE CAMINO* WITH ME?"

It was my third year of theology at the North American College in Rome. We had two weeks of Easter vacation to go experience Europe. A classmate and I decided to walk the *Camino Portugués*, a shorter version of the famous medieval pilgrimage route across Spain. (It's so famous that it's called simply *El Camino*, which means "the way" in Spanish.) I bought some shoes and borrowed a backpack, and we flew to Lisbon. We took a train to the Portuguese border and spent a week walking to the burial place of Saint James the apostle. Something special happened *on the way*. I started to see myself, and the ordinary world, in a whole new way. I discovered the magic of walking pilgrimages.

Three years later, I was back in America as a newly ordained priest. "We don't have to fly to Europe to walk down the road," I thought. I scoped out a walking route to a local shrine, lined up places to stay every twelve miles or so, and found people to bring us food each night. Twenty-two people joined me on that pilgrimage. Their lives were changed, and I realized that the magic of walking pilgrimages isn't limited to the plains of Spain. Every year for the past ten years, I've led a five-day walking pilgrimage to the Shrine of Our Lady of Good Help in Champion, Wisconsin. I never cease to come away with some new gift, blessing, or lesson learned on the way.

Walking pilgrimages are a much different experience from a bus pilgrimage. When you ride a bus to a shrine, it's mostly about the destination. Pilgrims look forward to a big "Aha" moment waiting for them when they arrive. Walking pilgrims, on the other hand, learn the joy of the journey. Familiar roads look differently when you travel them on foot. Pilgrims begin to appreciate the beauty around them. They enter into the ebb and flow of nature. They draw closer to the people they walk with. They learn to keep their eyes open for encounters with God along the way. Most of all, they learn to put one foot in front of the other and keep walking on good days and bad days. A walking pilgrimage is about more than the destination; it's a journey of the heart. It changes you in ways you never expected.

THE ADVENT JOURNEY

So, what does this have to do with Advent and Christmas? We all struggle with Advent. The Church is telling us to slow down, but the world is telling us, "Hurry up." We rush around preparing for the birth of Jesus. We look forward to the big "Aha" moment waiting for us at Christmas. And we always seem to miss out somehow. How is it that every year Christmas seems less merry and bright than we were hoping it would be? Too often, Christmas seems to fly by even more quickly than Advent does!

The problem is that we keep treating Advent like the bus on the way to Christmas. We expect to step off at Bethlehem and have some experience of Christmas spirit, some kind of "Aha" moment. The fact is that Holy Mother Church designed Advent to be more like a walking pilgrimage. You take a little step every day. You learn to enjoy the journey instead of rushing to Christmas — and then you're better prepared to enjoy the full Christmas season, rather than rushing through one day on your way to the new year. You connect with the people around you. You enter into a new rhythm. The ordinary things of life start to take on a new meaning. God meets you on the road. Think of this book as a Camino guidebook. It will show you how to step off the busy Christmas bus and walk the Advent road one day at a time. You will learn that Advent and Christmas are more than a destination; they involve a journey of the heart.

KEEP WALKING

This book lasts nearly ten weeks, from the first Sunday of Advent on November 27 to the feast of the Presentation on February 2. The feast of the Presentation (also called Candlemas) is the traditional final day after which Christmas decorations must be taken down. Using this book, you will get twenty-eight days to prepare for Christmas and forty days to celebrate Christmas (kind of like the forty days of Lent followed by the fifty days of Easter). We need those extra days. None of the people who saw the Christ Child in person understood the true meaning of Christmas. It was only in the days and years afterward that the "dawn from on high" began to rise in their hearts (cf. Lk 1:78). The same is true for us in our ongoing journey of faith. Praying with this devotional until February 2 will help you continue to see Jesus in the ordinary. Besides, it's easier to pray in the post-Christmas lull, and we need a little help getting through the low time in January.

You don't have to walk the whole way with me; it's your journey and you can quit any time. But let me encourage you to plan for a longer walk.

Consider putting up your Christmas tree a little later this year. Put on the lights and ornaments, but don't plug in the lights until the Light of the World is born on December 25. Then keep your tree lit all through the twelve days until January 6. Plan to keep at least your Advent wreath and Nativity scene up until February 2. It may seem like a long way to go now, but you'll be surprised at how quickly it passes. And you'll really enjoy those extra days.

IF YOU MISS A DAY

Even when you are too busy to pray, try to at least open this book and read the Scripture passage each day. If you end up missing a day or two (or even a week), don't try to go back and do all the meditations you missed. Just skip ahead to the current day and pray that one well. It is not important that you do every single meditation. What matters is that you put your heart into your prayer. Prayer is experiencing how our Father looks at you with love. Holiness is learning to live in his long, loving gaze every moment of your life.

NO ONE WALKS ALONE

You might assume because I wrote this book that I'm great at praying. Far from it! I was trained as a spiritual director through the Institute for Priestly Formation. I have taught countless numbers of people how to pray. I've been on pilgrimages and retreats and even a thirty-day silent retreat. But the truth is, unless I'm actually on a retreat or a pilgrimage, I usually pray badly. Most days I'm too busy, distracted, self-absorbed, or lazy to really pray well. And the problem is compounded during the busy Advent and Christmas season. I wrote this book because I need it too! I will be praying with you and for you this whole season. Please pray for me and for your fellow *Oriens* pilgrims. Consider joining me and Tracy Stewart from Our Sunday Visitor for a virtual Bible study each week. We will meet online to share our stories of the journey and encourage one another. Visit https://pilgrimpriest.us/book to learn more and sign up for free. We each make our own journey, and every journey is unique, but no one walks alone. ¡*Buen Camino!*

~ Fr. Joel Sember
Priest, Pastor, Pilgrim

Suggested Calendar for the Advent and Christmas Season

November 27, 1st Sunday of Advent: Light the first candle on your Advent wreath.

December 4, 2nd Sunday of Advent: Light the second candle on your Advent wreath.

December 6 (Tuesday): Give some treats for Saint Nicholas Day.

December 8 (Thursday): Solemnity of the Immaculate Conception. Put up your crèche (manger scene).

December 11, 3rd Sunday of Advent: Light the third (rose) candle on your Advent wreath.

December 13 (Tuesday): Do some research on traditions surrounding the feast of Saint Lucy.

Before December 25: Put up your Christmas tree. Decorate it, but don't plug the lights in. Wait until the Light of the World is born.

December 18, 4th Sunday of Advent: Light the fourth candle on your Advent wreath.

December 24/25: After attending Christmas Mass, put the baby Jesus in the crèche and light up your Christmas tree. Change the candles in your Advent wreath to white.

January 1 (Sunday): Octave Day of Christmas, solemnity of Mary, Mother of God. Start the new year with Mary.

January 6 (Friday): Epiphany. Have a family party to bless your home with blessed chalk. Afterward, you can take down the tree (if you want to) and the decorations, but don't take down the Advent wreath or the crèche.

January 23 (Monday): A day of penance in the United States in reparation for violations to the dignity of the human person committed through acts of abortion, and prayer for the full restoration of the legal guarantee to the right to life.

February 2 (Thursday): Feast of the Presentation. Have one last Christmas party! Light the candles on your wreath and have a family Candlemas procession to the crèche. Sing Christmas carols. Then put away any remaining Christmas decorations.

Blessing of an Advent Wreath

The use of the Advent Wreath is a traditional practice which has found its place in the Church as well as in the home. The blessing of an Advent Wreath takes place on the First Sunday of Advent or on the evening before the First Sunday of Advent. When the blessing of the Advent Wreath is celebrated in the home, it is appropriate that it be blessed by a parent or another member of the family.

All make the sign of the cross together: + In the name of the Father, and of the Son, and of the Holy Spirit.
Leader: Our help is in the name of the Lord.
Response: Who made heaven and earth.
Leader: A reading from the book of the Prophet Isaiah:

> *The people who walked in darkness*
> *   have seen a great light;*
> *Upon those who dwelt in the land of gloom*
> *   a light has shone.*
> *You have brought them abundant joy*
> *   and great rejoicing.*
> *As they rejoice before you as at the harvest,*
> *   as men make merry when dividing spoils.*
> *For a child is born to us, a son is given us;*
> *   upon his shoulder dominion rests.*
> *They name him Wonder-Counselor, God-Hero,*
> *   Father-Forever, Prince of Peace.*
> *His dominion is vast*
> *   and forever peaceful,*
> *From David's throne, and over his kingdom,*
> *   which he confirms and sustains*
> *By judgment and justice,*
> *   both now and forever. (Isaiah 9:1-2, 5-6)*

Leader: The Word of the Lord.
Response: Thanks be to God.

Leader: Let us pray.

> Lord our God,
> we praise you for your Son, Jesus Christ:
> he is Emmanuel, the hope of the peoples,
> he is the wisdom that teaches and guides us,
> he is the Savior of every nation.
>
> Lord God,
> let your blessing come upon us
> as we light the candles of this wreath.
> May the wreath and its light
> be signs of Christ's promise to bring us salvation.
> May he come quickly and not delay.
>
> We ask this through Christ our Lord.

Response: Amen.

The blessing may conclude with a verse from "O Come, O Come, Emmanuel":

> O come, desire of nations, bind
> in one the hearts of humankind.
> Bid ev'ry sad division cease,
> and be thyself our Prince of peace.
> Rejoice! Rejoice! Emmanuel
> shall come to thee, O Israel.

— From Book of Blessings

Week One

Lectio Divina

This first week we will use an ancient prayer form called *lectio divina* (pronounced LEK-si-o di-VEE-na). It has four simple steps, known by their Latin names: *lectio* (reading), *meditatio* (meditation), *oratio* (prayer), and *contemplatio* (contemplation). Don't worry about each Latin word. The prayer form is as simple as this: read, think, talk, listen.

We begin with a prayerful reading of a passage from Scripture. We turn over in our minds what we have read: What was the cultural context? What does this particular word mean? What does this mean to me? We chew on the passage for a while. Perhaps a particular word, phrase, or idea speaks to us. But it won't really be prayer if we just stay in our heads. So, we speak to God in our heart or out loud. A conversation takes two, so for the last part of *lectio*, we adopt an attitude of receiving. We are talking, then we are listening. Many people find the *contemplatio* to be a difficult step; they worry about if they are "doing it right" or "if it's really God" whose voice they hear. Don't try too hard. Just be quiet and receive for a little while. Prayer is not so much about getting something from God as it is just being with God. We are using Scripture as a conversation starter, but conversations with God go deeper than words. I'll walk you through it.

Grace of the Week: Each week has a particular theme or focus. The first week will focus on the creation of the world. The simplest things can be the easiest to forget, and the most profound when they are rediscovered. Pray for the grace to wonder anew at the marvel, mystery, and miracle of God's creation.

November 27 — Sunday
First Sunday of Advent

Happy Advent! Do you feel prepared to begin this journey? If you don't feel prepared, then you've come to the right place! Advent is a season of preparation. Doubtless you've heard the parable, "A journey of a thousand miles begins with a single step." By opening this book, you are taking the first step on your pilgrimage journey. As the journey continues, you will begin to see the importance of daily prayer. You may already have a great habit of daily prayer. Or you might be hoping to start a habit of daily prayer as part of *Oriens*. Let me review briefly the two ingredients that have helped me to pray well: place and time.

PLACE FOR PRAYER

Where will you pray? If you don't already have a prayer room or a prayer corner, make one. It can be a whole spare room, or as simple as a prayer chair or one side of a couch. Put distractions, like the remote and the mobile phone, out of reach. Hang some pictures or images or an inspiring Scripture quote. It doesn't have to be elaborate. It should be comfortable, free of distractions, and full of things that help you focus on God. Some people like to light a candle while they are praying (but do not leave candles unattended). Plan a *place* for prayer.

TIME FOR PRAYER

When will you pray? I like to pray right away when I get up in the morning. Some people most enjoy this book in the quiet of the evening. It may not happen exactly as you planned every day, but if you don't plan it, odds are it won't happen at all. We make time for the important things in our life, and prayer is the most important thing. Plan a *time* for prayer.

Lectio: Not unsurprisingly, *lectio divina* (divine reading) begins with a *reading* of the text. The Bible is God's word, once spoken through prophets and written by scribes. It has been passed down, copied again and again, and now rendered into English. Far from a dead letter, it continues to be very much alive through the presence and action of the Holy Spirit.

The Spirit intended them for the original audience that heard them spoken, and again as written prophecies referring to Jesus Christ, and again as words that you would read in this place and time in your life. These words have power. They have the power to touch hearts, change minds, and reveal mysteries. The Spirit has something to say to you today. Ask the Holy Spirit to help you receive the message that is meant for you. Then read the passage slowly and prayerfully.

ISAIAH 2:1–5 (LECTIONARY)

This is what Isaiah, son of Amoz,
saw concerning Judah and Jerusalem.
In days to come,
the mountain of the LORD's house
shall be established as the highest mountain
and raised above the hills.
All nations shall stream toward it;
many peoples shall come and say:
"Come, let us climb the LORD's mountain,
to the house of the God of Jacob,
That he may instruct us in his ways,
and we may walk in his paths."
For from Zion shall go forth instruction,
and the word of the LORD from Jerusalem.
He shall judge between the nations,
and impose terms on many peoples.
They shall beat their swords into plowshares
and their spears into pruning hooks;
one nation shall not raise the sword against another,
nor shall they train for war again.
O house of Jacob, come,
let us walk in the light of the LORD!

Meditatio: The mountain is a symbol of pilgrimage. As you climb a mountain, the ordinary hustle and bustle of the world fades below you. This is what prayer should do for you. Let the busyness of this overstuffed season fade for a little quiet time with the God who loves you.

What word, phrase, or idea stood out to you as you read the passage? Did something delight you, encourage you, or speak to you in a particular way? Do you desire peace, a little more quiet, instruction, or light? Read the passage again, slower this time, and notice the feelings or thoughts that come to you as you read.

Oratio: Now we speak to God. Christmas may seem a long way off (it is, in fact, twenty-eight days away, as this year's Christmas on a Sunday makes for the longest possible Advent). But I would venture to guess that you've had enough Christmases to know what a good one looks and feels like. Perhaps at this stage you desire the gifts wrapped earlier than ever, your family to all make it home, or perhaps just a better Christmas than last year. But let's look just a little bit deeper. Under the surface of Christmas and things going smoothly, what do you more deeply desire? What do you really want for Christmas? Ask yourself this question. Then turn to God in prayer. Speak to God the desire(s) of your heart. He's a good listener. This step happens best when your attention shifts from yourself and your reading of Scripture to the God who has been with you this whole time. You might picture yourself on top of the holy mountain, seated in God's house, with the light of God's presence shining upon you. Speak to him from your heart.

Contemplatio: After you've said your piece, read the passage a third time. As you read it, keep your attention fixed on God. See all the things that God desires to give his people: light, instruction, peace, unity ... What is it that God desires to give you? This time just receive for a few minutes. Don't try to imagine or invent what God might say. Just ask God, "What is on your heart for me? What is the gift you want to give me for Christmas?" Then be quiet with him and notice whatever emerges in your mind and heart. Spend a few minutes here in a quiet, contemplative mode before you move on. Just be, and be with the Lord, for a little while.

I often journal as I go, writing notes in the margins or in the journal space below. Throughout your *Oriens* journey, journaling is optional but highly encouraged. The "Suggestions for Journaling" each day are meant to help you pull more out of your meditation. You may not need them; you may have already journaled a small novel at this point. Or you may think nothing happened until you review the questions and realize that you did, in fact, have some kind of experience of God's presence. It's not a test, and these are not review questions. They are just here to help. Use whatever is helpful for you and ignore the rest.

SUGGESTIONS FOR JOURNALING

1. The thing I really love about Christmas is ...
2. The thing I really hate about Christmas, or found the most challenging about last Christmas, was ...
3. I get the most joy from ...
4. What do I want to make sure to do? What do I want to make sure not to do?
5. What is God's desire for my Christmas journey?
6. Where and when will I pray?
7. I most deeply desire ...

The most important part of our Advent journey is an attitude of thanksgiving. So, finish by saying "Thank You" to God for today's prayer time and close with an Our Father.

November 28 — Monday
Monday of the First Week of Advent

Preparation: *Come, Holy Spirit, enlighten the eyes of my heart* (see Ephesians 1:18).

Lectio: Ask God for the grace to wonder anew at the marvel, mystery, and miracle of creation. We must begin at the beginning. Which is exactly the place where the Bible chooses to begin. Thanks to modern science, we have a very different mental picture of the universe. In order to understand parts of this passage, we have to understand how the ancients saw the world. Picture a snow globe. It has a big dome over a heavy, stable base. Inside there are figures that experience snow when you shake the globe. Those figures are like us; we live inside the snow globe. Above our heads is a big blue dome called the sky. The stars are like ceiling ornaments stuck inside the dome. The sun and moon travel up one side and down the other. The dome has big floodgates that open to let rain or snow fall on us. Beneath our feet is the underworld, and beneath it all is the abyss, a sort of endlessly deep ocean. Who made the snow globe, and how did we get here? We're glad you asked. Read the Scripture passage through slowly and prayerfully, and ask to see this familiar Scripture with fresh eyes. Picture children seated around a campfire listening as a grandfather tells the ancient tale once again.

GENESIS 1:1–8

In the beginning, when God created the heavens and the earth — and the earth was without form or shape, with darkness over the abyss and a mighty wind sweeping over the waters —

Then God said: Let there be light, and there was light. God saw that the light was good. God then separated the light from the darkness. God called the light "day," and the darkness he called "night." Evening came, and morning followed — the first day.

Then God said: Let there be a dome in the middle of the waters, to separate one body of water from the other. God made the dome, and it separated the water below the dome from the water above the dome. And so it happened. God called the dome "sky." Evening came, and morning followed — the second day.

Meditatio: Despite the simplistic cosmology, the biblical author starts in exactly the same place as modern scientists do — with an explosion of light. All of the known matter and energy around us can be traced backward to a single point of expansion, the moment the Bible describes as "Let there be light." God speaks, and his will is done. His word becomes energy and matter, and a whole universe expands into existence and begins cooling into the sky that stretches above us. Scientists say that all the forces in the universe are perfectly balanced to allow our planet to exist. The Bible sees this as a result of careful design. Can you see the design in the universe around you? What must the Creator be like, if his creation is so amazing? Read the passage a second time.

Oratio: What do you think about all this? It might help to reflect on the last time you saw a beautiful sunrise, or were far enough from light pollution to catch a glimpse of the star-carpeted night sky. Picture the heavens stretching above us and the vast ocean beneath. Then speak to your Creator. Share with him your wonder at the creation that surrounds you.

Contemplatio: Read the passage one more time. Open your heart to receive whatever God might want to give you. Don't sweat this step. Contemplation is about resting in the mystery, being present to the God who is always present to you, and receiving whatever is in his heart for you. Be with the Lord for a few minutes before moving on to the next step.

SUGGESTIONS FOR JOURNALING
1. The part of today's prayer that most delighted me was …
2. I loved the image of …
3. My most noticeable thought or feeling was …

4. I struggled the most with …
5. The rest of the day (or tomorrow, if you pray at night), I plan to try to focus a little bit more on …

Spend a few minutes in wonder and awe at the mystery and marvel of creation that surrounds you! Let gratitude rise in your heart. Then close with an Our Father.

November 29 — Tuesday
Tuesday of the First Week of Advent

Preparation: *Come, Holy Spirit, enlighten the eyes of my heart.* Flip back and briefly review yesterday's prayer time. Start today's prayer with gratitude.

Lectio: Ask God to help you wonder anew at the marvel, mystery, and miracle of his creation. Read the passage below, slowly and prayerfully. Notice what jumps out to you as you read.

GENESIS 1:9–13
Then God said: Let the water under the sky be gathered into a single basin, so that the dry land may appear. And so it happened: the water under the sky was gathered into its basin, and the dry land appeared. God called the dry land "earth," and the basin of water he called "sea." God saw that it was good. Then God said: Let the earth bring forth vegetation: every kind of plant that bears seed and every kind of fruit tree on earth that bears fruit with its seed in it. And so it happened: the earth brought forth vegetation: every kind of plant that bears seed and every kind of fruit tree that bears fruit with its seed in it. God saw that it was good. Evening came, and morning followed — the third day.

Meditatio: God causes the water to recede until it forms into a giant ocean, covering everything except the pointy bits that are above "sea level." At this point, life begins in the form of all kinds of vegetation. Picture a green planet teeming with an abundance of different forms of plant life. Plants are already complex enough to have a reproductive system and to create seeds, which spread throughout the world. Each plant is brilliantly designed and beautiful in its own way. What do you think as you watch God creating? Why do you think he is doing this? Read the passage again prayerfully.

*Oratio***:** Scientists still do not fully understand photosynthesis. It allows plants to extract energy from the sun and store it in a way that other creatures are able to use. The energy in the coal that powers much of our electricity and in the gasoline that fuels our cars was originally captured from the sun by hard-working plants. Without plants, no complex life forms would be possible. Think of how often we take for granted the contribution plants make to our lives. What else do we take for granted about the world around us? Thank God for all the greenery and speak to him with gratitude. Then read the passage one more time.

*Contemplatio***:** The God who made the universe, and is so often taken for granted, enjoys spending time with you. Just open your heart to receive whatever is in God's heart for you — his kindness, mercy, generosity. Spend a few minutes with your maker before moving on.

SUGGESTIONS FOR JOURNALING
1. What are some of the simple but important things that I tend to take for granted?
2. How have I been ungrateful?
3. I am most grateful for …
4. I felt God saying to me …
5. I left prayer wanting …

God is the source of life, but he is often taken for granted. After you've journaled, spend a minute in gratitude for the prayer time you've just had. Then close with an Our Father.

Wednesday of the First Week of Advent

SAINT ANDREW, APOSTLE

Andrew is most famous for introducing his brother Simon Peter to Jesus (see Jn 1:35–42). Andrew is said to have preached the Gospel in Greece, where he suffered martyrdom at Patras. Bound by ropes to an X-shaped cross, he preached to the crowds for two days until he was overcome by death. He is the patron of Greece, Scotland, and Russia. The white X on the flag of the United Kingdom (the "Union Jack") comes from Saint Andrew. There is a tradition of beginning a Christmas novena on his feast day.

Preparation: *Come, Holy Spirit, enlighten the eyes of my heart.* Flip back to yesterday's prayer and recall a blessing you experienced. Spend a minute picturing the expanse of the sky above and the teeming green-and-blue earth beneath. Let gratitude rise in your heart.

Lectio: In your own words, ask God to help you wonder anew at the marvel, mystery, and miracle of his creation. Read today's passage slowly and prayerfully. As you do, picture in your mind the myriad creatures that surround us: giant whales and clever squids, soaring birds and flying insects, bears in their dens and birds in the trees.

GENESIS 1:20–25

Then God said: Let the water teem with an abundance of living creatures, and on the earth let birds fly beneath the dome of the sky. God created the great sea monsters and all kinds of crawling living creatures with which the water teems, and all kinds of winged birds. God saw that it was good, and God blessed them, saying: Be fertile, multiply, and fill the water of the seas; and let the birds multiply on the earth. Evening came, and morning followed — the fifth day.

Then God said: Let the earth bring forth every kind of living creature: tame animals, crawling things, and every kind of wild animal. And so it happened: God made every kind of wild animal, every kind of tame animal, and every kind of thing that crawls on the ground. God saw that it was good.

Meditatio: Think of the incredible variety of animals that fill the world. There are birds that swim and fish that fly, and insects of every shape and size. Each creature is uniquely adapted to its own ecosystem. All the different species rely on one another in a delicate balance of predator, prey, and prey's prey. And it all starts with plants. What is your favorite kind of animal? What do you find creepy? Each one has its purpose and its place. Read the passage again slowly.

Oratio: We are surrounded with an abundance we can't even fathom. Scientists think that over 80 percent of the world's species, and 90 percent of the world's ocean creatures, have yet to be discovered and classified. And yet, species are going extinct at an alarming rate. We might ever know only a tiny fraction of God's creation. How does this make you feel? What does it tell you about God? What part of creation do you most enjoy, and what part do you find uncomfortable or pointless? Thank God for his creation and share your thoughts with the Creator. When you are done talking, read the passage one more time.

Contemplatio: You have spoken; now take time to listen. Receive what God wants to say to you and how God wants to respond to you. Perhaps you receive nothing more than a feeling of peace or presence. Whatever it is, spend a few minutes in silence before you move on.

SUGGESTIONS FOR JOURNALING

1. When it comes to the animals around me, I most enjoy …
2. I am humbled by the realization that …
3. I have a hard time fathoming …
4. I would like someone to explain to me …
5. I ended prayer wanting …

After you've journaled, close with a brief conversation giving thanks to God for your prayer experience. Then close with the Saint Andrew Novena Prayer:

Hail and blessed be the hour and moment in which the Son of God was born of the most pure Virgin Mary, at midnight, in Bethlehem, in the piercing cold. In that hour vouchsafe, I beseech Thee, O my God, to hear my prayer and grant my desires, [here mention your request] through the merits of Our Savior Jesus Christ, and of His blessed Mother. Amen.

December 1 — Thursday
Thursday of the First Week of Advent

Preparation: *Come, Holy Spirit, enlighten the eyes of my heart.* How has God's love been manifest to you in your prayer time so far? Spend a minute savoring God's loving care for all his creatures and especially his care for you. Let gratitude rise in your heart.

Lectio: In your own words, ask God to help you wonder anew at the marvel, mystery, and miracle of creation. After filling the earth with all kinds of various creatures, God still has one more creature to make: You. Read the passage slowly and prayerfully.

GENESIS 1:26–31

Then God said: Let us make human beings in our image, after our likeness. Let them have dominion over the fish of the sea, the birds of the air, the tame animals, all the wild animals, and all the creatures that crawl on the earth.

> *God created mankind in his image;*
> *in the image of God he created them;*
> *male and female he created them.*

God blessed them and God said to them: Be fertile and multiply; fill the earth and subdue it. Have dominion over the fish of the sea, the birds of the air, and all the living things that crawl on the earth. God also said: See, I give you every seed-bearing plant on all the earth and every tree that has seed-bearing fruit on it to be your food; and to all the wild animals, all the birds of the air, and all the living creatures that crawl on the earth, I give all the green plants for food. And so it happened. God looked at everything he had made, and found it very good. Evening came, and morning followed — the sixth day.

Meditatio: God steps back, as it were, and pauses to think. This final creature will be like all the rest of the animals in important ways, including the fact that it exists as male and female. But it will have two special characteristics: It will be made in the image and likeness of God, and it will exercise dominion over the rest of the animals. In what ways are human beings like God? Why would God choose to create a creature like himself? Read the passage a second time.

Oratio: What does it feel like to have dominion over all the other creatures? Every human being is utterly unique. We each have a unique combination of facial features, physical characteristics, personality, and mental abilities. Your unique combination of genetic code and gene expression (phenotype) never existed before you were conceived, and it will never exist again in the world. You are like all the other creatures and all the other humans, but you are also utterly unique. You are the only *you* that God has ever and will ever make. What thoughts, feelings, or desires are rising in your heart? Turn to the God who made you. Share with him what is on your heart. Be completely honest with him. When you have poured out your heart, read the passage a third time slowly and prayerfully.

Contemplatio: Let God look at you. Creation was not complete without you. God sees you as "very good." Receive what God wants to share with you, what is in his heart for you. Rest in his love for you for a few minutes before moving on.

SUGGESTIONS FOR JOURNALING
1. I exercise dominion over God's creatures when …
2. What is special about me?
3. I saw the image and likeness of God shining in another human being when …
4. I have a hard time accepting that …
5. I sensed God wanting me to know …
6. My deepest desire right now is for …

After you've journaled, close with a conversation with God giving thanks for creating you and for listening to you in prayer today. Then pray an Our Father.

December 2 — Friday
Friday of the First Week of Advent

Preparation: *Come, Holy Spirit, enlighten the eyes of my heart.* Think back on yesterday's prayer time (or the last time you prayed if you missed yesterday). How was the experience a blessing for you? Spend a minute being grateful for God's presence and for the things you are learning and the ways you are growing.

Lectio: In your own words, ask God to help you wonder anew at the marvel, mystery, and miracle of his creation. The creation around us comes from God, and it points to God. The marvels of creation are signs of God's wisdom, genius, and care. Can you look beyond creation and catch sight of its Creator? Read the passage slowly and prayerfully. Notice whatever word, phrase, or idea jumps out at you.

PSALM 145

I will extol you, my God and king;
*   I will bless your name forever and ever.*
Every day I will bless you;
*   I will praise your name forever and ever.*
Great is the LORD and worthy of much praise,
*   whose grandeur is beyond understanding.*
One generation praises your deeds to the next
*   and proclaims your mighty works.*
They speak of the splendor of your majestic glory,
*   tell of your wonderful deeds.*
They speak of the power of your awesome acts
*   and recount your great deeds.*
They celebrate your abounding goodness
*   and joyfully sing of your justice.*
The LORD is gracious and merciful,
*   slow to anger and abounding in mercy.*

The LORD is good to all,
    compassionate toward all your works.
All your works give you thanks, LORD,
    and your faithful bless you.
They speak of the glory of your reign
    and tell of your mighty works,
Making known to the sons of men your mighty acts,
    the majestic glory of your rule.
Your reign is a reign for all ages,
    your dominion for all generations.
The LORD is trustworthy in all his words,
    and loving in all his works.
The LORD supports all who are falling
    and raises up all who are bowed down.
The eyes of all look hopefully to you;
    you give them their food in due season.
You open wide your hand
    and satisfy the desire of every living thing.
The LORD is just in all his ways,
    merciful in all his works.
The LORD is near to all who call upon him,
    to all who call upon him in truth.
He fulfills the desire of those who fear him;
    he hears their cry and saves them.
The LORD watches over all who love him,
    but all the wicked he destroys.
My mouth will speak the praises of the LORD;
    all flesh will bless his holy name forever and ever.

Meditatio: The proper response of a creature is to praise God. Saint Augustine tells us that the plants, birds, fish, sun, moon, and stars all praise God simply by being what they were made to be and doing what they were made to do. What were we made to be? What was I made to do? Human beings alone can choose to worship God or choose to ignore his presence. We can never stop being the image of God, but our choices make us more like God or more distant from God. Read the passage again slowly, or focus on the word, phrase, or idea that jumped out at you from the first reading.

Oratio: Have you experienced that the Lord is gracious and merciful? Have you had prayers answered? Previous generations, your parents and grandparents, aunts and uncles, spoke the praises of God. Now it is your turn. Speak up, join your voices to the voices of your ancestors and to the voices of all the creatures, and praise God from your heart. If there is something that is blocking you from praising God, some obstacle, doubt, or hurt, then talk to God about it. When you are done, read the passage a third time.

Contemplatio: Your praise resounds and echoes into the distance. What does God want to say to you, or give you, in response to the praise you have given him? Maybe it is a thought, word, or feeling. Just spend a few minutes letting God look at you with love and gazing back at him. Enjoy the presence of God before you move on.

SUGGESTIONS FOR JOURNALING

1. God is worthy of much praise. Do I make the praise of God part of my daily routine?
2. I am most grateful for …
3. How did the previous generation, my parents and grandparents, aunts and uncles, speak the praises of God?
4. How has the Lord been near to me when I called upon him?
5. I experienced the mercy of God when …
6. I most deeply desire …

_____

_____

_____

_____

_____

_____

_____

_____

_____

_____

_____

_____

_____

_____

_____

_____

After you've journaled, close with a conversation with God giving thanks for your prayer experience. You may be tempted to skip this step, as you have already been praising and thanking God. It is really important that you begin and end prayer with a spirit of gratitude. Think of it like having coffee with a friend. When you meet up with your friend, you greet them warmly with a hug, a handshake, or kind words. At the end of a conversation, you thank your friend for spending time with you. You wouldn't just get up and walk away. So, spend a minute in thanksgiving before you say goodbye for now. Then pray an Our Father.

December 3 — Saturday
Saturday of the First Week of Advent

SAINT FRANCIS XAVIER

Francis was the third son born to a noble family in Navarre, now Northern Spain, in 1506. As often happened with the younger sons of nobles, he was destined for an ecclesiastical career and sent to the University of Paris. His college roommate was St. Ignatius of Loyola, who was fifteen years older than he and had undergone a profound religious conversion. Francis was won over by Ignatius and became one of the seven founding members of the Society of Jesus (the Jesuits). He was sent to preach the Gospel in the Orient. For ten years he labored tirelessly, bringing more than 30,000 souls to the light of Christ. His travels took him to India and Japan, and he died on the doorstep of China. How might God be calling you to something greater than your family's plans for you?

REVIEW

Preparation: *Come, Holy Spirit, enlighten the eyes of my heart.* Instead of spending time with a new passage, we will pray with the passages that most spoke to you in this past week. Saint Ignatius called this kind of prayer time a *repetition*. The idea behind a repetition is not so much to do a prayer passage all over again, but to go back to the place you most noticed God's presence and felt loved by God. You return to that place in order to deepen the encounter and the conversation with God. Flip back through your past week's journal entries. Notice what emerged in the conversations. Here are some questions to help you:

1. The prayer time that I enjoyed most and got the most out of was ...
2. The prayer time I really struggled with was ... What made it hard for me?
3. Where did I notice the presence of God? What did his presence feel like, or how did it affect me?

4. What was God doing, saying, or giving me this week?
5. How did I respond to what God was doing?
6. I'm most grateful for …

7. Is there an image or experience of God's loving presence that emerged from my prayer during this first week? Or was there a word, phrase, or message that really touched me?

Savor that image of God's loving presence. Rest there for a few minutes. Then thank God for today's prayer time and end with an Our Father.

Week Two

Imaginative Prayer

How did *lectio divina* go? If you found yourself struggling, here are a couple of thoughts.

First, don't try too hard. We often think we have to "do prayer right" in order to get something from God. When we put the burden on ourselves, we really aren't open to receive. And receiving isn't hard work. The work comes when we have to let go of our expectations that prayer will happen only if I figure out how to "pray well." In reality, prayer is just noticing and focusing on the presence and action of God in your life. God is present and active all the time. He doesn't talk only during one little part of prayer, and he doesn't stop talking just because you ended your prayer time. Many people find that they receive an answer to their prayer during Mass or before bedtime or at some other moment during the day. The secret is to have an attitude of willingness to receive from God whenever he might be communicating with us.

Secondly, remember that the goal is not to have nice notes in your journal. The goal is quality time with the God who loves you. If you've spent any quality time with God this past week, you've done well. Be careful not to judge your prayer too much. Just be grateful for the first week.

And if you didn't pray at all last week, that's OK. Life gets away from us sometimes. Just pick up with today's prayer and start here.

This week we will learn a new prayer form called imaginative prayer. St. Ignatius of Loyola was the pioneer of this prayer form. He stumbled onto it quite by accident. It changed his life, and he went on to use it to help change other people's lives. Some people are skeptical of this prayer form. They fear it is just creating fantasy air castles. You certainly could do that, but that wouldn't be prayer time. Prayer is about connecting with the God who loves you and is present with you right now. Most of us are only vaguely aware of God's presence. We are much more aware of our current location in space and time, what happened yesterday, and what is on our calendar for today. These are passing things that we need to temporarily unplug from if we want to connect more deeply with God.

A good book or movie will take you out of the present moment for a while and move you to another place and time. In doing so, it can help you connect with something deeper: your own hopes and dreams, your fears, your potential, and what it means to be part of the human condition. In a similar way, imaginative prayer helps connect you with the deeper reality of God's loving presence that is silently behind and beyond all space and time. The imagination is only a conversation starter. Again, if you spend quality time with God, you have achieved your goal.

Grace of the Week: We are surrounded by God's creation. But we are also creatures, created by God the Father and made for a relationship with him. However, we have fallen out of relationship with him. The human race is so used to being separated from God that we have nearly forgotten that we were made by God and for God. Ask God in your own words for the grace to feel the pain of separation from God so as to desire more strongly a deeper relationship with him.

December 4 — Sunday
Second Sunday of Advent

Preparation: *Come, Holy Spirit, enlighten the eyes of my heart.* Start your prayer with gratitude. Turn back to yesterday and look at the image of God's loving care for you that emerged in your review time. Use your imagination to picture that moment again. Spend about a minute just resting in that experience and savoring the unconditional love with which God loves you.

Set the Scene: Ask God in your own words for the grace to feel the pain of separation from God so as to desire more strongly a deeper relationship with him. Read the passage below. As you do, set the scene in your mind. Picture the Jordan River winding its way through the desert. Picture the large crowds gathering to listen to this roughly clothed man preach repentance and then get dunked in waters of repentance. Picture the fine clothing of the Pharisees and Sadducees who are also coming for a show of righteousness, but getting less than a warm welcome.

MATTHEW 3:1-12 (LECTIONARY)

John the Baptist appeared, preaching in the desert of Judea and saying, "Repent, for the kingdom of heaven is at hand!" It was of him that the prophet Isaiah had spoken when he said:

> *A voice of one crying out in the desert,*
> *Prepare the way of the Lord,*
> *make straight his paths.*

John wore clothing made of camel's hair and had a leather belt around his waist. His food was locusts and wild honey. At that time Jerusalem, all Judea, and the whole region around the Jordan were going out to him and were being baptized by him in the Jordan River as they acknowledged their sins.

When he saw many of the Pharisees and Sadducees coming to his baptism, he said to them, "You brood of vipers! Who warned you to flee from the coming wrath? Produce good fruit as evidence of your repentance. And do not presume to say to yourselves, 'We have Abraham as our father.' For I tell you, God can raise up children to Abraham from these stones. Even now the ax lies at the root of the trees. Therefore every tree that does not bear good fruit will be cut down and thrown into the fire. I am baptizing you with water, for repentance, but the one who is coming after me is mightier than I. I am not worthy to carry his sandals. He will baptize you with the Holy Spirit and fire. His winnowing fan is in his hand. He will clear his threshing floor and gather his wheat into his barn, but the chaff he will burn with unquenchable fire."

Action! See the face of John the Baptist as he preaches in the spirit and power of Elijah. Picture the faces of the people in the crowd as they acknowledge their sins. Picture the faces of the Pharisees and Sadducees as John singles them out and takes them to task. They aren't used to this kind of treatment. Feel the tension in the air. Who will back down first? Read the passage a second time.

Acknowledge: As you process this scene, notice what is happening in you. What part of the passage do you find most intriguing? What thoughts or feelings are going on inside of you as you picture this passage? Where do you find yourself in the scene?

Relate: Turn to God and share with him what is on your heart. This can be a more challenging part of the prayer. Think of it this way: You are watching John the Baptist preaching repentance. You notice someone is standing next to you on the shores of the Jordan River. You look over and recognize the face of Jesus. He has been watching too. Talk to him about what you see, feel, and think.

Receive: Now turn to Jesus, look at him, and let him look at you. How does he respond to what you have shared? What is in his heart for you? What does he want to say to you or want you to notice? How is he being moved by the face of each person that you imagined earlier? Read the passage a third time, or perhaps just the part that you feel most drawn to. As you do, focus on God and let him speak to you, or just quietly receive what he wants to give you.

Respond: This part is about continuing the conversation. You have shared, you have received something from God, and now you respond to what he gave you. Perhaps you received a sense of peace, and you should say, "Thank you." Or maybe you sensed his care for each person and also for you, and you are moved to realize how much our Lord cares. Now just receive his care. I'm offering a couple of thoughts only to show you that it's a simple process, like chatting with a friend. Just be with the Lord and savor his loving presence for a minute or two before moving on.

SUGGESTIONS FOR JOURNALING

1. While imagining the scene, what stood out to me was …
2. My strongest thought or feeling during the meditation was …
3. I sensed God communicating to me …
4. I had a sense of joy when …
5. I ended my prayer with a deeper desire for …

After you've journaled, end with prayer. Spend a minute thanking God for your prayer experience. Then pray an Our Father.

December 5 — Monday
Monday of the Second Week of Advent

Preparation: *Come, Holy Spirit, enlighten the eyes of my heart.* Call to mind a recent experience of God's loving care. Spend about a minute just resting in that experience and savoring the unconditional love with which God loves you. Let gratitude rise in your heart.

Set the Scene: Ask God in your own words for the grace to feel the pain of separation from God so as to desire more strongly a deeper relationship with him. Read through the passage and set the scene in your mind. The Bible tells us that the world has become corrupt as a result of human sin. Picture God looking down on the earth and watching wars, theft, adultery, murder, abuse of power, and lies of every kind. Each sin leads to more sin in a descending spiral of corruption. All of creation is becoming corrupted by man's sinfulness. God has had enough; he is going to wash the world clean. I would suggest picturing the scene not so much as God dictating to Noah, but more like an epiphany moment. Noah has a very clear sense of what God is calling him to do, and he knows that he needs to act now.

GENESIS 6:12–22

When God saw how corrupt the earth had become, since all mortals had corrupted their ways on earth, God said to Noah: I see that the end of all mortals has come, for the earth is full of lawlessness because of them. So I am going to destroy them with the earth.

Make yourself an ark of gopherwood, equip the ark with various compartments, and cover it inside and out with pitch. This is how you shall build it: the length of the ark will be three hundred cubits, its width fifty cubits, and its height thirty cubits. Make an opening for daylight and finish the ark a cubit above it. Put the ark's entrance on its side; you will make it with bottom, second and third decks. I, on my part, am about to bring the flood waters on the earth, to destroy all creatures under the sky in which there is the breath of life; everything on earth shall perish. I will establish my covenant with you. You shall go into the ark, you and your sons, your wife and your sons' wives with you. Of all living creatures you shall bring two of every kind into the ark, one male and one female, to keep them alive along with you. Of every kind of bird, of every kind of animal, and of every kind of thing that crawls on the ground, two of each will come to you, that you may keep them alive. Moreover, you are to provide yourself with all the food that is to be eaten, and store it away, that it may serve as provisions for you and for them. Noah complied; he did just as God had commanded him.

Action! No one will listen to God except Noah; he alone knows that disaster is coming upon the face of the earth. What would that feel like? Imagine what Noah was thinking and feeling as he went about completing the task God had given him. Read the passage a second time.

Acknowledge: "Noah found favor with the Lord;" he was righteous and blameless in his generation (Genesis 6:8 and 9b). Are you open to receive what God wants to give you? God desires to rescue you. Are you listening and responding to God's call? What are you thinking and feeling as you picture the scene?

Relate: Do you fear what God might ask you to do? Are you asking, but not receiving anything from God? Turn to God and share with him what is on your heart. Speak to God honestly whatever you might be thinking or feeling.

Receive: How does God respond to you? Receive whatever it is that God wants to give you — a thought, a word, a feeling, or just a sense of peace or presence. Don't try too hard. Read the passage a third time.

Respond: Whatever you have received from God, respond to it. If you received nothing, be patient. Tell God you will wait, or tell him about your frustration. Know that God loves you and he is with you even if you're not feeling it at this very moment. Just be with God for a minute or two before moving on.

SUGGESTIONS FOR JOURNALING

1. While picturing the scene, I was most struck by …
2. I had a hard time imagining that …
3. My strongest thought, feeling, or desire was …
4. The thing I noticed about Noah was …
5. The presence of God with me seemed to say to me …
6. I ended prayer with a sense that …

After you've journaled, close with a brief conversation giving thanks to God for your prayer experience. Then pray an Our Father.

December 6 — Tuesday
Tuesday of the Second Week of Advent

SAINT NICHOLAS, BISHOP

Saint Nicholas was the bishop of Myra in modern-day Turkey. He died on this day around AD 350. Very little is known of him apart from the legends that were passed down. It is said that a poor man had three daughters. He had no money to furnish dowries for them and therefore they had no possibility of honorable marriages. Nicholas went secretly at night and threw a bag of gold into the home, then another. The father caught him with the third bag and was finally able to identify his benefactor. There is a tradition of children leaving their shoes out on the eve of his feast and finding them miraculously full of treats, most notably oranges. Practice a little extra generosity today.

Preparation: *Come, Holy Spirit, enlighten the eyes of my heart.* Call to mind your recent experience of God's loving care. Spend about a minute just resting in that experience and savoring the unconditional love of the Father for his child. Let gratitude rise in your heart.

Set the Scene: Ask God in your own words for the grace to feel the pain of separation from God so as to desire more strongly a deeper relationship with him. We have plenty for our imagination. There's a boat full of animals, a giant flood, and Noah is six hundred years old! All the biblical accounts through Genesis 11 are a kind of prehistory of the world, after which human lifespans get more realistic. We shouldn't read this as a literal blow-by-blow historic account of exactly how it happened. Most human civilizations have passed on a great flood story. Even Native Americans have a version involving a brave hero who saved the animals in a canoe. We want to tap into the sense that human wickedness has destabilized the world to the point that all life is now under threat. God, however, has set a plan in motion to rescue his creation and the people who will listen to him. Read the passage and set the scene in your mind.

GENESIS 7:11–14,17–21

In the six hundredth year of Noah's life, in the second month, on the seventeenth day of the month: on that day

All the fountains of the great abyss burst forth, and the floodgates of the sky were opened.

For forty days and forty nights heavy rain poured down on the earth.

On the very same day, Noah and his sons Shem, Ham, and Japheth, and Noah's wife, and the three wives of Noah's sons had entered the ark, together with every kind of wild animal, every kind of tame animal, every kind of crawling thing that crawls on the earth, and every kind of bird.

The flood continued upon the earth for forty days. As the waters increased, they lifted the ark, so that it rose above the earth. The waters swelled and increased greatly on the earth, but the ark floated on the surface of the waters. Higher and higher on the earth the waters swelled, until all the highest mountains under the heavens were submerged. The waters swelled fifteen cubits higher than the submerged mountains. All creatures that moved on earth perished: birds, tame animals, wild animals, and all that teemed on the earth, as well as all humankind.

Action! Picture the relentless rain, followed by the unstoppable rising flood waters. Even with all our modern technology, rain and floods continue to be mostly out of our control. Every year you can watch dramatic and scary videos of floods occurring in various places in the world, carrying away everything in their path. There is nothing a hapless world can do to save itself from this climate-induced catastrophe. Noah, however, had been listening to God and long ago began taking the necessary steps. How does Noah feel? How does the rest of humanity feel? Read the passage again.

Acknowledge: What do you feel as you watch this scene of primordial destruction unfold? You might feel relief, injustice, or foreboding, or even anger. Name your feelings, but receive them without judging them. What thoughts go through your mind?

Relate: Turn to God and share with him what is in your heart — your thoughts, feelings, and desires. Be honest with God, even if you find yourself angry at God. Share your thoughts honestly.

Receive: We probably notice all the death and destruction, but the Bible is keen to point out that God saved the ones he was able to save. How did God feel as he watched the disaster unfold? What was in his heart for Noah and the people of Noah's day? How does God respond to what you have just shared with him? What is in his heart for you? Perhaps you have a hard time looking at God, or receiving what God wants to say to you. Don't be afraid of God's response, but also don't try too hard. Look at God with the eyes of your heart, and let God look at you. Read the passage a third time, or just the part that spoke to you.

Respond: Whatever it is that God has given you, respond to it. The point here is to keep the conversation going until you've said what you needed to say, and received whatever God wanted to give you. Just be with God for a minute or two before moving on.

SUGGESTIONS FOR JOURNALING

1. We've all heard this story before, but praying with it made me realize that …
2. My strongest thought, feeling, or desire was …
3. I told God that …
4. Through God's eyes, I saw differently that …
5. I received a new insight or understanding …
6. I ended prayer wanting …

After you've journaled, close with a brief conversation giving thanks to God for your prayer experience. Then pray an Our Father.

After you've journaled, close with a brief conversation giving thanks to God for your prayer experience. Then pray an Our Father.

December 7 — Wednesday
Wednesday of the Second Week of Advent

Preparation: *Come, Holy Spirit, enlighten the eyes of my heart.* Call to mind a recent experience of God's loving care. Spend about a minute just resting in that experience and savoring the unconditional love with which God loves you. Let gratitude rise in your heart.

Set the Scene: Ask God in your own words for the grace to feel the pain of separation from God so as to desire more strongly a deeper relationship with him. Earth has been washed clean, and humanity and creation are given a fresh start. We see allusions to the original creation story in the words, "Be fertile and multiply and fill the earth" (see Gn 1:28). Human beings are allowed to eat animals, whereas prior to this point they were only given plants to eat (see Gn 1:29). It is at this point that animals begin to fear human beings. Human beings are not allowed to kill other human beings, except for capital punishment. Read the passage through and set the scene in your mind.

GENESIS 8:18—9:6

So Noah came out, together with his sons and his wife and his sons' wives; and all the animals, all the birds, and all the crawling creatures that crawl on the earth went out of the ark by families.

Then Noah built an altar to the LORD, and choosing from every clean animal and every clean bird, he offered burnt offerings on the altar. When the LORD smelled the sweet odor, the LORD said to himself: Never again will I curse the ground because of human beings, since the desires of the human heart are evil from youth; nor will I ever again strike down every living being, as I have done.

All the days of the earth,

> seedtime and harvest,
> cold and heat,
> Summer and winter,
> and day and night
> shall not cease.

God blessed Noah and his sons and said to them: Be fertile and multiply and fill the earth. Fear and dread of you shall come upon all the animals of the earth and all the birds of the air, upon all the creatures that move about on the ground and all the fishes of the sea; into your power they are delivered. Any living creature that moves about shall be yours to eat; I give them all to you as I did the green plants. Only meat with its lifeblood still in it you shall not eat.

Indeed for your own lifeblood I will demand an accounting: from every animal I will demand it, and from a human being, each one for the blood of another, I will demand an accounting for human life.

> Anyone who sheds the blood of a human being,
> by a human being shall that one's blood be shed;
> For in the image of God
> have human beings been made.

Action! There is a sense of fresh start, of a return to a better spiritual and physical state. The earth is clean again, the animals are saved, and humans can start over. Human beings continue to have evil in their hearts, an evil that could lead to murder and therefore the need for capital punishment. Those who, instead of guarding against evil in their hearts, nurture evil and do evil will need to be pruned from among us. It's a harsh but necessary means to keep things from spiraling out of control. Read the passage again.

Acknowledge: Notice what stirs up inside of you: thoughts, feelings, desires. God promises not to wipe out the whole human race again with a flood. But that doesn't give us a free pass; he is still concerned about human capacity for evil and still sets limits on human activity. "I'll be watching you" might as well have been the words at the end of this passage. How does that make you feel?

Relate: Turn your heart to God and speak to him. Share with God what this passage stirred up within you. Now let him look at you with love. How does he respond?

Receive: Read the passage a third time. This time receive whatever is in God's heart for you — his thoughts, feelings, desires. How does it make God suffer when he sees his children hurting one another? What does he want for his children? Don't think too hard about this step. Just notice what comes up in the prayer.

Respond: Receive what God has to give you. Then respond in some way. Perhaps you need to say, "I'm sorry." Perhaps God is inviting you to some kind of action. Be with the Lord for a minute or two before moving on.

SUGGESTIONS FOR JOURNALING

1. A new insight or understanding I received was …
2. I felt convicted that …
3. I sensed God communicating to me …
4. I see sin in a new and different light …
5. I ended prayer wanting …

After you've journaled, close with a brief conversation giving thanks to God for your prayer experience. Then pray an Our Father.

December 8 — Thursday
Solemnity of the Immaculate Conception

The Church has long believed that the Blessed Virgin Mary was preserved free from all sin starting at the very moment of her conception. Christians have celebrated this feast for over 1,200 years, but it was officially declared a dogma by Blessed Pope Pius IX in 1854. Four years later, Our Lady appeared to Saint Bernadette at Lourdes, France, and told her, "I am the Immaculate Conception." Today's feast is a holy day of obligation for Catholics, and the Gloria is sung at Mass.

Preparation: *Come, Holy Spirit, enlighten the eyes of my heart.* Call to mind God's loving care for you and spend about a minute just resting in that experience and savoring the unconditional love God has for you. Let gratitude rise in your heart.

Set the Scene: Ask God in your own words for the grace to feel the pain of separation from God so as to desire more strongly a deeper relationship with him. Ephesus is a city in Asia Minor where Saint Paul had labored for two years to preach the Gospel (Acts 19:10). His letter to them emphasizes the unity of the Church in Christ, who has united both Jews and Gentiles into one body. Picture Saint Paul writing this introduction to his letter. He is reflecting on how God called him from Judaism to Christianity, and how God then called his hearers from their pagan ways to join him in the new Christian religion. He reflects on the people from Ephesus that he has come to know and love. His words are full of gratitude.

EPHESIANS 1:3–6, 11–12 (LECTIONARY)
Brothers and sisters:
Blessed be the God and Father of our Lord Jesus Christ,
who has blessed us in Christ
with every spiritual blessing in the heavens,

as he chose us in him, before the foundation of the world,
to be holy and without blemish before him.
In love he destined us for adoption to himself through Jesus
    Christ,
in accord with the favor of his will,
for the praise of the glory of his grace
that he granted us in the beloved.

In him we were also chosen,
destined in accord with the purpose of the One
who accomplishes all things according to the intention of
    his will,
so that we might exist for the praise of his glory,
we who first hoped in Christ.

Action! Do you realize that you, too, were chosen "before the foundation of the world"? Have you felt yourself adopted as a child of God? When have you hoped in Christ? Read the passage again and let gratitude fill your heart.

Acknowledge: How does it feel to be destined, chosen, and adopted? The Immaculate Conception, which we celebrate today, was given to Mary precisely so that Jesus could be born for you and save you from your sins. He made Mary immaculate so that you, too, could be made immaculate. God put even more work into rescuing you than he did into rescuing Noah and creation from the flood! Sort through what is going on inside of you. Notice your strongest thought, feeling, or desire. Is there a word or phrase that stood out to you?

Relate: God, your secret benefactor, has been unfolding your salvation since before the Big Bang. He is here with you right now. What do you want to say to him? Speak to him in your heart. Share with him what this passage stirred up within you. Just be honest. When you are finished sorting and sharing your feelings, read the passage a third time.

Receive: What does God want to say to you? What is in his heart for you? Don't sweat this step. Many times God gives something simple like a feeling of peace, a sense of his presence, or a sense that he understands what we are going through.

Respond: Continue the conversation for a few minutes, then just be present to the Lord, and let him be present to you for a few minutes before moving on.

SUGGESTIONS FOR JOURNALING

1. The word, phrase, or idea from this passage that most spoke to me was …
2. I was surprised to realize that …
3. My strongest thought, feeling, or desire was …
4. I saw with new eyes …
5. I ended prayer with a deeper sense that …

_____

_____

_____

_____

_____

_____

_____

_____

_____

_____

_____

_____

_____

_____

_____

_____

_____

_____

_____

After you've journaled, close with a brief conversation giving thanks to God for your prayer experience. Then close with a Hail Mary.

December 9 — Friday
Friday of the Second Week of Advent

SAINT JUAN DIEGO

On this day in 1532, a native Aztec man was on his way to Mass when he heard a voice calling his name. A beautiful woman was standing on the hill of Tepeyac near present-day Mexico City. She told him that she was the ever-Virgin Mother of the true God. She wanted him to go speak to the bishop and ask that a church be built on that place so she could manifest her love for all people. The bishop was skeptical and sent Juan Diego back to ask the lady for a sign. However, that night his uncle took sick. He cared for him until it seemed that the end was near, then he ran to get a priest for the anointing of the sick. He tried to avoid the lady by going the other way around the hill, but then he saw her coming down the hill to meet him. She told him not to worry about his uncle, then sent him up the hill to pick some roses, which miraculously were blooming in the December cold. She arranged them with her own hands in his *tilma* (a kind of poncho made of cactus fiber) and then sent him to town saying he should show the sign to no one but the bishop himself.

Preparation: *Come, Holy Spirit, enlighten the eyes of my heart.* Call to mind an image of God's loving care for you that has emerged in your prayer. Spend about a minute just resting in that experience and savoring the unconditional love with which God loves you. Let gratitude rise in your heart.

Set the Scene: This is Joshua's final discourse to the people of Israel, after they have defeated the city of Jericho and settled in the promised land. Though the Jewish people have seen God do great things, they are surrounded by pagan nations that worship many gods. Joshua wants to leave them with a final exhortation to listen to the one true God. Read the passage slowly and prayerfully.

73

JOSHUA 24:1-2A, 3-7AB, 11, 13-15

Joshua gathered together all the tribes of Israel at Shechem, summoning the elders, leaders, judges, and officers of Israel. When they stood in ranks before God, Joshua addressed all the people: "Thus says the LORD, the God of Israel: I brought your father Abraham from the region beyond the River and led him through the entire land of Canaan. I made his descendants numerous, and gave him Isaac. To Isaac I gave Jacob and Esau. To Esau I assigned the mountain region of Seir to possess, while Jacob and his children went down to Egypt.

"Then I sent Moses and Aaron, and struck Egypt with the plagues and wonders that I wrought in her midst. Afterward I led you out. And when I led your ancestors out of Egypt, you came to the sea, and the Egyptians pursued your ancestors to the Red Sea with chariots and charioteers. When they cried out to the LORD, he put darkness between you and the Egyptians, upon whom he brought the sea so that it covered them. Your eyes saw what I did to Egypt. "Once you crossed the Jordan and came to Jericho, the citizens of Jericho fought against you, but I delivered them also into your power. I gave you a land you did not till and cities you did not build, to dwell in; you ate of vineyards and olive groves you did not plant.

"Now, therefore, fear the LORD and serve him completely and sincerely. Cast out the gods your ancestors served beyond the River and in Egypt, and serve the LORD. If it is displeasing to you to serve the LORD, choose today whom you will serve, the gods your ancestors served beyond the River or the gods of the Amorites in whose country you are dwelling. As for me and my household, we will serve the LORD."

Action! As the Israelites stand before Joshua, some may have foreign idols hidden in their tents or amulets under their clothing. These other gods promised fertility, success in war, riches, and many other blessings.

It's not such an easy choice to part with them. Imagine the struggle going on in each heart and in each family. How faithful are you to the true God? How faithful do you want to be? Read the passage again.

Acknowledge: Juan Diego grew up with the Aztec gods. Fed by human sacrifice, they promised the people victory and prosperity. He had made the brave choice to abandon his ancestral gods to follow the God preached by the Spanish friars. What was that choice like for him? Is God really first in your life, or have you allowed other things to take the first place? Notice your thoughts, feelings, and desires.

Relate: God is listening as Joshua invites the people to this covenant ritual. He recounts all the wonderful deeds God has done for them. Though they owe God a debt they can never repay, God does not want slaves, but sons. God has done great things for you, but God will let you walk away if you choose not to serve him. He values your freedom. In fact, he created it as a gift for you. How will you use your freedom? Speak to him in your heart. Share with God whom you have decided to serve. If you have questions or fears or difficulties, don't be afraid to share those with God as well.

Receive: Read the passage a third time, or just read the part that speaks to you. Be open to what God wants to say to you, without fear or expectation. Perhaps you will be reminded of a previous commitment, of God's mercy, or he will give you a sense of peace or confidence in his presence. Just notice whatever thought, feeling, or desire comes back to you in response to your honesty.

Respond: Converse with the Lord for a minute or two, and then spend a few minutes savoring his merciful love for you and all the great things he has done for you.

SUGGESTIONS FOR JOURNALING
1. I felt convicted by …
2. The word, phrase, or idea that most spoke to me was …
3. I see the love of God in a new way …

4. I feel that God is calling me to …
5. My biggest obstacle to following God wholeheartedly is …
6. God wanted me to know …
7. I ended prayer with a stronger desire for …

After you've journaled, close with a brief conversation giving thanks to God for your prayer experience. Then pray an Our Father.

Saturday of the Second Week of Advent

REVIEW

Preparation: *Come, Holy Spirit, enlighten the eyes of my heart.* Call to mind an image of God's loving care for you that has emerged in your prayer. Spend about a minute just resting in that experience and savoring the unconditional love with which God loves you. Let gratitude rise in your heart.

This past week, we started with John the Baptist, survived the flood with Noah, saw the Mother of God with Juan Diego, and then were challenged by Joshua if we were really going to be faithful to the true God. Flip back through your past week's journal entries. As you do, notice what emerged in the conversation. Here are some questions to help you:

1. Where did I notice God, and what was he doing or saying?
2. How did I respond to what God was doing?
3. I really struggled with …
4. Prayer really seemed to click when …
5. I'm grateful for …
6. Now at the end of this Second Week of Advent, what new meaning or purpose is emerging from my Advent pilgrimage? Perhaps go back and look at your very first day's prayer time and see what God seems to be wanting from your Advent pilgrimage.

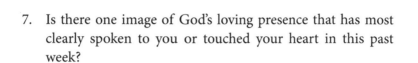

7. Is there one image of God's loving presence that has most clearly spoken to you or touched your heart in this past week?

Conclude by conversing with God about your week. **Acknowledge** what you have been experiencing. **Relate** it to him. **Receive** what he wants to give you. **Respond** to him. Then savor that image of God's loving presence and rest there for a minute or two. Close with an Our Father.

Week Three

The Secret to a Better Advent

How was imaginative prayer? Some people love it, and some people struggle with it. *Lectio divina* can be used with any Scripture passage, but imaginative prayer works best with passages that contain visuals and action. As we move forward, I'll use one or the other prayer form each day, depending on what I think fits with the passage. You don't have to follow my guidance, though. If you prefer one prayer form, you can use it all the time. But let me encourage you to try to become comfortable with either prayer form. Keep in mind that the goal is not nice notes in your journal or amazing imaginative experiences. These two prayer forms are just conversation starters; it is the conversation itself that is key to a good prayer time. Good prayer is about spending quality time with God. If you have spent quality time with God at all this week, you have done well.

MAKING SPACE FOR GOD

If you're having a hard time with consistent prayer, I want to remind you of the importance of time and place (p. 22). Do you have a dedicated prayer space, prayer corner, or prayer chair? Even just one half of a couch will do, as long as you are intentional about making the side-table into a space that helps you pray.

What time have you picked for prayer? Is it realistic? If you plan to get up earlier each day, then you need to be going to bed earlier, and also praying a little before bed. How we end our day strongly impacts how the next day begins. If you plan to pray in the evenings, you need to set an alarm for yourself, and be willing to stop other things or even cut out habits if they keep you from prayer. These are practical ways of literally and figuratively "making space" for God in your life. Your relationship with God can't be just "one more thing" in your life; he has to take priority over other things. Your attempts to pray consistently will be more successful if you consciously give God a space in your home and a time on your schedule.

MAKING SPACE FOR CHRISTMAS

One of the first spiritual experiences I can recall is childhood memories of Christmas disappointment. I always got the presents I dreamed of and more, but the reality of new gifts was somehow less than the anticipation had been. That started me on a quest for a better Christmas. Our world ends its Christmas celebration on the day of Jesus' birth, while Catholics aren't supposed to start celebrating until his birthday. Trying to observe Advent, however, makes one feel cheated out of Christmas. Eventually I discovered the eight days of Christmas (the octave), the twelve days of Christmas (to January 6, the Epiphany), and the forty days of Christmas (ending on February 2, the feast of the Presentation). Marking these extra feast days allows us to carve out time for Christmas. Believe me, Advent "works" when Christmas lasts forty days. I have come to really enjoy waiting to light the Christmas tree and then savoring it as long as it lasts into January. Don't feel bad if you've already been playing Christmas music since before Thanksgiving. Just try a little Christmas in January this year and see what you think of it.

Grace of the Week: God has a plan to restore creation and undo the effects of sin. We need a savior, and God has just the thing. We will pray with Scripture passages that give us examples of faith to inspire us and prepare us for the final nine-day countdown to Christmas. Ask God for the grace of humility and littleness so that he can unfold his will in your life with all its power and glory.

December 11— Sunday
Third Sunday of Advent

Preparation: *Come, Holy Spirit, enlighten the eyes of my heart.* Be present to the God who is always present to you. Call to mind his loving care for you and spend the first minute of your prayer just resting in the free, unearned gift of loving and being loved. Let gratitude rise in your heart.

Set the Scene: Pray for the grace of humility and littleness so that God can unfold his will in your life with all its power and glory. John the Baptist appears again; perhaps flip back to last Sunday's reading (pp. 53–54), or just recall how you imagined the scene. John has not seen any of the works of Jesus with his own eyes. After baptizing the Messiah in Matthew chapter 3, John is subsequently arrested (see Mt 4:12). Picture him holed up in a dank prison in the basement of Herod's castle. Rumors of Jesus' miracles have come to John, and he sends his disciples to ask Jesus the all-important question. Read the passage and set the scene in your mind.

MATTHEW 11:2–11 (LECTIONARY)
When John the Baptist heard in prison of the works of the
    Christ,
he sent his disciples to Jesus with this question,
"Are you the one who is to come,
or should we look for another?"
Jesus said to them in reply,
"Go and tell John what you hear and see:
the blind regain their sight,
the lame walk,
lepers are cleansed,
the deaf hear,
the dead are raised,
and the poor have the good news proclaimed to them.
And blessed is the one who takes no offense at me."
    As they were going off,
Jesus began to speak to the crowds about John,

"What did you go out to the desert to see?
A reed swayed by the wind?
Then what did you go out to see?
Someone dressed in fine clothing?
Those who wear fine clothing are in royal palaces.
Then why did you go out? To see a prophet?
Yes, I tell you, and more than a prophet.
This is the one about whom it is written:
> *Behold, I am sending my messenger ahead of you;*
> *he will prepare your way before you.*
Amen, I say to you,
among those born of women
there has been none greater than John the Baptist;
yet the least in the kingdom of heaven is greater than he."

Action! Is John having doubts? He predicted a messiah mightier than himself, saying, "He will clear his threshing floor and gather his wheat into his barn, but the chaff he will burn with unquenchable fire" (Mt 3:12). Jesus has turned out rather meek and mild in comparison. On the other hand, perhaps John's faith is stronger than ever, and he wants to encourage his disciples to transfer their allegiance to Jesus. Picture the crowd gathered around Jesus and listening intently as the disciples arrive with their question. Read the passage again.

Acknowledge: Perhaps your Advent pilgrimage is not going as you had hoped. Perhaps you feel behind in your Christmas preparations. Have you found yourself discouraged with a lack of results, or prayer times that were missed or did not go according to plan? When have you felt disappointed with yourself, the events in the world, the Church, even God himself? Listen to your feelings and acknowledge them.

Relate: Jesus is listening intently to you. Speak to him what is on your heart — your thoughts, feelings, or desires. How does Jesus receive what you want to say to him? He already knows, and he's been waiting for you to ask. Let him look at you with love.

Receive: What is in Jesus' heart for you? Perhaps he responds with another question, like he does in today's Gospel. Perhaps he invites you to a different way of seeing your situation, or reminds you of something you had forgotten. It's your turn to listen and receive. Read the passage a third time.

Respond: The conversation continues, or perhaps you are comfortable just sitting with the Lord. Can you receive his love for you? Do you still have your doubts? Talk and listen, back and forth, for as long as you need to. Now just be with the Lord for a minute or two before moving on.

SUGGESTIONS FOR JOURNALING

1. While imagining the scene, what stood out to me was ...
2. I struggle to accept the fact that ...
3. I sensed God communicating to me ...
4. I feel God calling me to a new way of thinking or acting ...
5. I ended prayer with a deeper sense that ...

_____

_____

_____

_____

_____

_____

_____

_____

_____

_____

_____

_____

_____

_____

_____

_____

_____

_____

_____

_____

After you've journaled, close with a brief conversation giving thanks to God for your prayer experience. Then pray an Our Father.

December 12 — Monday
Our Lady of Guadalupe

On December 12, 1532, the native called Juan Diego arrived at the bishop's palace clutching something in his *tilma*. He refused to show it to anyone but the bishop. The bishop's servants made him wait for a long time before finally ushering him into the bishop's room. He unfolded his mantle, and Castilian roses tumbled out onto the floor. Even more surprisingly, a miraculous image of the lady herself was imprinted on his *tilma*. The bishop and his entourage accompanied him to check on his uncle, who turned out to be in perfect health after he, too, received a visit from the beautiful lady. A shrine was built in which to house the miraculous image, and next to it a little house for Juan Diego. He spent the rest of his life telling his story as millions of native Aztecs converted to the Catholic Faith. The image hangs today in the shrine of Our Lady of Guadalupe on the outskirts of Mexico City. It testifies to her love for all people, including you.

Preparation: *Come, Holy Spirit, enlighten the eyes of my heart.* Be present to the God who is always present to you. Call to mind his loving care for you and spend the first minute of your prayer just resting in the free, unearned gift of loving and being loved. Let gratitude rise in your heart.

Set the scene: Pray for the grace of humility and littleness so that God can unfold his will in your life with all its power and glory. Today's Scripture passage is taken from the Book of Revelation. It is a dramatic and imaginative vision of the struggle between good and evil. Read the passage once to set the scene in your mind.

REVELATION 11:19A; 12:1–6A, 10AB (LECTIONARY)

God's temple in heaven was opened,
and the ark of his covenant could be seen in the temple.

A great sign appeared in the sky, a woman clothed with
the sun,

with the moon under her feet,
and on her head a crown of twelve stars.
She was with child and wailed aloud in pain as she labored
    to give birth.
Then another sign appeared in the sky;
it was a huge red dragon, with seven heads and ten horns,
and on its heads were seven diadems.
Its tail swept away a third of the stars in the sky
and hurled them down to the earth.
Then the dragon stood before the woman about to give
    birth,
to devour her child when she gave birth.
She gave birth to a son, a male child,
destined to rule all the nations with an iron rod.
Her child was caught up to God and his throne.
The woman herself fled into the desert
where she had a place prepared by God.

Then I heard a loud voice in heaven say:
"Now have salvation and power come,
and the Kingdom of our God
and the authority of his Anointed."

Action: This passage is taken from today's feast day. The image left on Juan Diego's *tilma* shows a woman standing in front of the sun, with the moon under her feet, and wearing a blue-green cloak covered in stars. The sun and moon represented the most powerful Aztec gods. Our Lady is claiming to be more powerful than they are. Yet, she herself is not a god, as she is shown with head bowed and hands folded, reverently praying to God. She is pregnant with God's child. Read the passage again.

Acknowledge: What do you think and feel as you picture the scene? What is the woman feeling? The woman and her child are not afraid to be humble and little, as God protects them and provides for them. Does the thought of humbleness and littleness make you uncomfortable? Do you have a hard time trusting in God's care and protection?

Relate: Where do you see God in today's Scripture passage? Turn to God and speak to him. Share your thoughts, feelings, and desires, the things that were stirred up by today's prayer time.

Receive: Let God respond to what you have shared. Notice whatever thought, feeling, or desire God wants to communicate to you. Read the passage a third time.

Respond: Receive whatever new way God invites you to see this scene in Revelation, the woman, or your own life. Make room in your heart for God's way of seeing things. Then rest in God's love for you for a few minutes before moving on.

SUGGESTIONS FOR JOURNALING

1. I was surprised by …
2. I have a hard time believing that …
3. When I hear the words *humble* and *little*, I think of …
4. I have a newfound appreciation for …
5. I feel God calling me to a new way of seeing, thinking, or acting …

After you've journaled, close with a brief conversation giving thanks to God for your prayer experience. Then pray a Hail Mary.

December 13 — Tuesday
Tuesday of the Third Week of Advent

SAINT LUCY, MARTYR

Little is known about this young Christian girl from Syracuse in Sicily. It is said that a disappointed suiter denounced her as a Christian, and she was executed in AD 304. She is one of the seven women mentioned by name in the Roman Canon of the Mass (Eucharistic Prayer I). Her name comes from the Latin word *lux,* meaning "light." Because of this, she is the patroness of eyesight. Her feast day is celebrated with the lighting of candles and special foods, particularly in Scandinavian countries. Pray that God will enlighten your heart so as to make you a light for others.

Preparation: *Come, Holy Spirit, enlighten the eyes of my heart.* Call to mind God's loving presence and spend the first minute of your prayer just resting in the free, unearned gift of loving and being loved. Let gratitude rise in your heart.

Lectio: Ask God in your own words for the grace of humility and littleness so that God can unfold his will in your life with all its power and glory. The letter to the Hebrews wants to show us that faith is the ticket to a life that pleases God. We often think of faith in terms of what we believe. We use phrases like, "Teaching the Faith," or, "He knows the Faith." But the biblical sense of faith is better understood along the lines of faithfulness or trustworthiness. Abel, Enoch, and Noah were faithful to God. They themselves trusted God. They listened to God and did his will, which in turn made them trustworthy. They trusted God, and God could trust them. Read the passage slowly and prayerfully.

HEBREWS 11:1–7

Faith is the realization of what is hoped for and evidence of things not seen. Because of it the ancients were well attested. By faith we understand that the universe was ordered by the word of God, so that what is visible came into being through the invisible. By faith Abel offered to God a sacrifice greater than Cain's. Through this he was attested to be righteous, God bearing witness to his gifts, and through this, though dead, he still speaks. By faith Enoch was taken up so that he should not see death, and "he was found no more because God had taken him." Before he was taken up, he was attested to have pleased God. But without faith it is impossible to please him, for anyone who approaches God must believe that he exists and that he rewards those who seek him. By faith Noah, warned about what was not yet seen, with reverence built an ark for the salvation of his household. Through this he condemned the world and inherited the righteousness that comes through faith.

Meditatio: You have to know someone in order to really trust them. Faith springs from a personal relationship. By "personal," I don't mean private (not a "personal" pan pizza), but rather a relationship between persons (like receiving a "personal" message). What is the personal message God wants to send you? How is God inviting you to trust him more deeply? Read the passage a second time.

Oratio: Notice the thoughts, feelings, and desires that are rising within you. Do you find it hard to trust God? Are you doubting his faithfulness? Do you not feel that you, yourself, are trustworthy? Do you doubt that God would want a relationship with you? Or do you find yourself grateful for the gift of faith, asking that it increase, celebrating people you know who have faith? Read the passage a third time, but this time focus on the work that God did in and through those who trusted him.

Contemplatio: Continue to focus on God. Receive his love for you and whatever he wants to give you. Just be with the Lord for a minute or two and allow your faith to increase before moving on.

SUGGESTIONS FOR JOURNALING

1. I could add to the list of Abel, Enoch, and Noah with people (family, friends, and fellow church members) who I know personally, in particular …

2. I want to trust God, but I feel that he let me down when …

3. I have a hard time believing God would put his trust in me because …

4. My faith in God grew when …

5. The personal message God had for me was …

_____

_____

_____

_____

_____

_____

_____

_____

_____

_____

_____

_____

_____

_____

_____

_____

_____

_____

After you've journaled, close with a brief conversation giving thanks to God for your prayer experience. Then pray an Our Father.

December 14 — Wednesday

Wednesday of the Third Week of Advent

Preparation: *Come, Holy Spirit, enlighten the eyes of my heart.* Remind your heart of God's loving presence. Spend the first minute of your prayer just resting in the free, unearned gift of loving and being loved. Let gratitude rise in your heart.

Lectio: Ask God for the grace of humility and littleness so that he can unfold his will in your life with all its power and glory. The city of Jerusalem has just survived an attack from a competing power. The king, Ahaz, fears another attack. God sends the Prophet Isaiah to reassure the king that God will be taking care of the situation. Read the passage slowly and prayerfully.

ISAIAH 7:10–14 (LECTIONARY — FOURTH SUNDAY OF ADVENT, YEAR A)

> *The LORD spoke to Ahaz, saying:*
> *Ask for a sign from the LORD, your God;*
> *let it be deep as Sheol, or high as the sky!*
> *But Ahaz answered,*
> *"I will not ask! I will not tempt the LORD!"*
> *Then Isaiah said:*
> *Listen, O house of David!*
> *Is it not enough that you weary people?*
> *must you also weary my God?*
> *Therefore the Lord himself will give you this sign;*
> *the virgin shall conceive, and bear a son,*
> *and shall name him Emmanuel.*

Meditatio: Ahaz is a descendant of King David and an ancestor to Jesus Christ (see Mt 1:9). His seemingly humble response is hiding his fear and his unwillingness to trust in God's providence. When have you been afraid to trust in God's providence? How is God inviting you to a deeper trust in him? Read the passage again.

Oratio: In the original context, God is promising prosperity for Israel and destruction of her enemies (see Is 7:15–16). The early Christians believed it was also meant as a prophecy that a future descendant of the House of David would be born of a virgin, and would himself be Emmanuel, God-with-us. God wants to give the king more than he is willing to ask for. God wanted to give the world a greater gift than we could have ever imagined. What do you really want this Christmas? Share your desires with God.

Contemplatio: It is likely that God wants to give you far more than you are prepared to ask for. In fact, God wants to be "God-with-you" and to share his very self with you. Open your heart to receive the gift that God wants to give you in your prayer time today. Then spend a few minutes resting in his loving presence with you right here and now.

SUGGESTIONS FOR JOURNALING

1. I am afraid to ask God for what I really want because …
2. I have experienced Emmanuel, God-with-me, when …
3. The greatest gift of my Advent journey so far has been …
4. God seemed to want to give me …
5. I ended prayer wanting …

After you've journaled, close with a brief conversation giving thanks to God for your prayer experience. Then pray an Our Father.

December 15 — Thursday
Thursday of the Third Week of Advent

Preparation: *Come, Holy Spirit, enlighten the eyes of my heart.* Be present to the God who is always present to you. Call to mind his loving care for you and spend the first minute of your prayer just resting in the free, unearned gift of loving and being loved. Let gratitude rise in your heart.

Lectio: In your own words, ask for the grace of humility and littleness so that God can unfold his will in your life with all its power and glory. Yesterday, we read Isaiah's prophecy of a virgin birth. Four chapters later, the prophet shares more of the story. Jesse was the father of King David. A future offspring of Jesse will bring so much peace that even the animals will not harm each other. Read the passage slowly and picture the scene in your mind.

ISAIAH 11:1–10 (LECTIONARY — SECOND SUNDAY OF ADVENT, YEAR A)

> On that day, a shoot shall sprout from the stump of Jesse,
> and from his roots a bud shall blossom.
> The spirit of the LORD shall rest upon him:
> a spirit of wisdom and of understanding,
> a spirit of counsel and of strength,
> a spirit of knowledge and of fear of the LORD,
> and his delight shall be the fear of the LORD.
> Not by appearance shall he judge,
> nor by hearsay shall he decide,
> but he shall judge the poor with justice,
> and decide aright for the land's afflicted.
> He shall strike the ruthless with the rod of his mouth,
> and with the breath of his lips he shall slay the wicked.
> Justice shall be the band around his waist,

and faithfulness a belt upon his hips.
Then the wolf shall be a guest of the lamb,
and the leopard shall lie down with the kid;
the calf and the young lion shall browse together,
with a little child to guide them.
The cow and the bear shall be neighbors,
together their young shall rest;
the lion shall eat hay like the ox.
The baby shall play by the cobra's den,
and the child lay his hand on the adder's lair.
They shall not harm or ruin on all my holy mountain;
for the earth shall be filled with knowledge of the LORD,
as water covers the sea.
On that day, the root of Jesse,
set up as a signal for the nations,
the Gentiles shall seek out,
for his dwelling shall be glorious.

Meditatio: We now realize that this prophecy refers to the kingdom of heaven. The justice and peace that God intends to bring upon the earth will only be fully established in heaven. We are sometimes tempted to think that the Messiah still has work to do because we haven't seen wolves and lambs make peace yet. However, the unfinished business lies not so much within the world as within each of us. Jesus wants to bring his peace and his justice into your heart. Consider the transformation God longs to work *within* you. Do you really believe that his plans for you are good? Do you believe he has the power to accomplish those plans? Read the passage again.

Oratio: At this very moment, the Lord is in your midst. As always, he is listening to you. Are you cooperating with his work of peace and justice, or getting in the way? Do you really want his power to unfold in your life, or do you fear that you will be slayed by the breath of his lips? Seek him out and speak to him honestly and openly.

Contemplatio: Read the passage a third time. Now enter into an attitude of receiving. What does God desire to give you? What is he calling you to? Spend a few minutes just receiving the loving gaze of God and being with God. Good prayer is really just quality time with God.

SUGGESTIONS FOR JOURNALING

1. The thing that most struck me about this passage was …
2. I was troubled by …
3. I was encouraged by …
4. What is the work that I need the Messiah to do in my life?
5. What is the work that the Messiah is asking me to do to bring peace, reconciliation, or justice to the world around me in a concrete way?

After you've journaled, close with a brief conversation giving thanks to God for your prayer experience. Then pray an Our Father.

Friday of the Third Week of Advent

REVIEW

We're doing our review one day early. Tomorrow, December 17, begins the final nine days of preparation for Christmas. We will switch over to the daily Mass readings as they begin to unfold the story of the birth of Jesus Christ. Let us pause for a moment and review our week.

Preparation: *Come, Holy Spirit, enlighten the eyes of my heart.* Be present to the God who is always present to you. Call to mind his loving care for you and spend the first minute of your prayer just resting in the free, unearned gift of loving and being loved. Let gratitude rise in your heart.

This past week we looked at faith in God. Flip back through your past week's journal entries. As you do, notice what emerged in the conversation. Here are some questions to help you:

1. Where did I notice God, and what was he doing or saying?
2. How did I respond to what God was doing?
3. I really struggled with …
4. Prayer really seemed to click when …
5. I'm grateful for …
6. This week, God seemed to be trying to communicate to me …

Now go back and review the past reviews from Saturday, December 3 (p. 45), and Saturday, December 10 (p. 78).

1. How has God been answering the prayers that I was praying and the struggles I was having in the early days of our prayer pilgrimage?
2. God seems to be giving me …
3. Upon further review, it turns out I really wanted … for Christmas.
4. So far, the most clear and touching image of God's love for me has been …

_____

_____

_____

_____

_____

_____

_____

_____

_____

_____

_____

_____

_____

_____

_____

_____

_____

Conclude by conversing with God about your review. **Acknowledge** what you have been experiencing. **Relate** it to him. **Receive** what he wants to give you. **Respond** to him. Then savor that image of God's loving presence and rest there for a minute or two. Close with an Our Father.

December 17 — Saturday
Countdown to Christmas: Nine

O Wisdom of our God Most High,
guiding creation with power and love:
come to teach us the path of knowledge!

Nine days before Christmas, the Advent season switches gears. The lectionary provides readings from the Gospel passages that immediately precede the birth of Jesus. Each day is assigned a special "O Antiphon," poetic invocations that draw on Old Testament prophecies, which foretell who the coming Messiah is and what he will do. We will pray with the daily lectionary readings now until Christmas. These Gospel passages from Matthew and Luke will be familiar to you. Perhaps you even prayed with them last year. As you pray with them again, you will begin to see the genius of the liturgical year. We return to the same Scriptures and feasts as last year, but they aren't the same experience the next time around. New insights and spiritual experiences build on the previous year's experiences. God is, as Saint Augustine said, "Ever ancient, ever new." Let's see what new things God has in store for you this year.

Preparation: *Come, Holy Spirit, enlighten the eyes of my heart.* Be present to the God who is always present to you. Call to mind his loving care for you and spend the first minute of your prayer just resting in the free, unearned gift of loving and being loved. Let gratitude rise in your heart.

Lectio: Ask God for the grace of humility and littleness so that he can unfold his will in your life with all its power and glory. Read the passage slowly and prayerfully. Underline the names you recognize as you go along.

MATTHEW 1:1–17 (LECTIONARY)

The book of the genealogy of Jesus Christ,
the son of David, the son of Abraham.

Abraham became the father of Isaac,
Isaac the father of Jacob,
Jacob the father of Judah and his brothers.
Judah became the father of Perez and Zerah,
whose mother was Tamar.
Perez became the father of Hezron,
Hezron the father of Ram,
Ram the father of Amminadab.
Amminadab became the father of Nahshon,
Nahshon the father of Salmon,
Salmon the father of Boaz,
whose mother was Rahab.
Boaz became the father of Obed,
whose mother was Ruth.
Obed became the father of Jesse,
Jesse the father of David the king.

David became the father of Solomon,
whose mother had been the wife of Uriah.
Solomon became the father of Rehoboam,
Rehoboam the father of Abijah,
Abijah the father of Asaph.
Asaph became the father of Jehoshaphat,
Jehoshaphat the father of Joram,
Joram the father of Uzziah.
Uzziah became the father of Jotham,
Jotham the father of Ahaz,
Ahaz the father of Hezekiah.
Hezekiah became the father of Manasseh,
Manasseh the father of Amos,
Amos the father of Josiah.
Josiah became the father of Jechoniah and his brothers

at the time of the Babylonian exile.

After the Babylonian exile,
Jechoniah became the father of Shealtiel,
Shealtiel the father of Zerubbabel,
Zerubbabel the father of Abiud.
Abiud became the father of Eliakim,
Eliakim the father of Azor,
Azor the father of Zadok.
Zadok became the father of Achim,
Achim the father of Eliud,
Eliud the father of Eleazar.
Eleazar became the father of Matthan,
Matthan the father of Jacob,
Jacob the father of Joseph, the husband of Mary.
Of her was born Jesus who is called the Christ.

Thus the total number of generations
from Abraham to David
is fourteen generations;
from David to the Babylonian exile, fourteen generations;
from the Babylonian exile to the Christ,
fourteen generations.

Meditatio: We often roll our eyes at the biblical genealogy because of the unpronounceable names. But these were real people who really lived. You may not know all these names, but God knows every single person on this list, and they are all precious to him. The remains of each one are buried somewhere here on earth, and God knows the resting place of them all. Some of them were famous saints and others are rather infamous. The lineage of the Messiah is just as messy as your family history and mine (see Gn 38). Yet, each one is an important link in an unbroken chain of ancestors that would give birth to God's Son. If there had been no Abiud, there would have been no Jesus. All along, he was guiding creation with power and love. What does your bloodline look like? How might God be using you, your family, and other apparently ordinary people to play a part in his extraordinary plans? Reflect for a few minutes, then read the passage again slowly. Notice your thoughts and feelings and the part that most speaks to you.

Oratio: Do you question your value? Do you wonder if God really has a plan? Do you sometimes feel insignificant or a burden to others? Share your thoughts, feelings, and desires with the God who created you. Be honest with him.

Contemplatio: Read the passage again, or just the part that spoke to you. Open your heart to receive what God wants to give you. Your life is a precious link in the chain of humanity. Receive whatever God wants to show you or give you: a word, image, or thought. But maybe you also will have a bit of a conversation. God is with you in this ordinary moment. You matter to him. Rest in and savor his love for you.

SUGGESTIONS FOR JOURNALING

1. I see God's hand in my own personal history when …
2. Because of my family or past, I struggle with …
3. I sensed God communicating to me …
4. I see my family history in a new light …
5. Optional: Write out your own genealogy after the style of this Scripture passage. Spend time praying for each of your ancestors.

_____

_____

_____

_____

_____

_____

_____

_____

_____

_____

_____

_____

_____

_____

_____

_____

_____

_____

_____

_____

_____

_____

After you've journaled, close with a brief conversation of thanksgiving to God for today's prayer time. Then pray an Our Father.

Week Four

Making Prayer Happen When You Get Busy

Half an hour's meditation each day is essential, except when you are busy. Then a full hour is needed.

— *St. Francis de Sales*

It seems that my Advent always follows the same pattern. The first week or two, I find the season to be surprisingly enjoyable. I remark that I don't feel rushed this year and I look forward, finally, to a peaceful and prayerful Christmas. Then everything hits at once — Christmas cards start to pile up, I realize I still have to send cards, I haven't bought gifts, and now last-minute planning for the Christmas season is upon me. My general habit is to freak out, get angry, and mutter under my breath, "I hate this season. Bah, humbug!"

One year when I became so overwhelmed, I quit trying at all. I just sat in my prayer space and prayed a full, solid holy hour. I may have gone a few minutes over the hour; since I wasn't going to catch up, what difference did it make? Then I wandered over to the office and, to my surprise, accomplished far more than I ever thought possible. This is the paradox of prayer. When I focus on the work, instead of God, the work piles up. When I focus on God, instead of the work, the work gets done.

That is why I encourage you not to try to catch up if you miss a day. Or a week. Or are finally opening the book for the first time today. *Oriens* shouldn't be yet another thing that piles up. Rather, I want you to see it as an invitation to quiet time with the Lord. When you approach it with the right attitude, you never really "fall behind" on *Oriens*.

One of the devil's most successful temptations is to distract people for a day or two so they don't remember to pick up *Oriens*. Then when they finally remember to pray, the enemy whispers, "Oh well, you failed. You might as well give up now. You could try again next year." You wouldn't believe how many people fall for this little trick. There's also the daily trick: "I only have a few minutes now, so instead of praying, I'll focus on the things that are piling up, and wait to pray until I get some of those things done first." You can guess what happens next. That's right, you never catch up.

If you do fall a few days behind, do this: Read the Grace of the Week for the week you are on. Then turn to today's meditation and pray for today. You're all caught up! The goal is quality time with God, not getting every prayer prayed or making nice notes in your journal.

That having been said, the more you are able to open the book each day, the more you will benefit from the pilgrimage. Any prayer time in a day, however small, is a victory. Even just opening the book before bed and reading the Scripture passage for that day is a victory. We are on a prayer pilgrimage. If you just keep walking, even baby steps will eventually get you to your destination.

Grace of the Week: This week we will continue through the days of the Christmas countdown. Let us open our hearts to our King, who humbled himself to free all men and women from sin, Satan, and death. Ask God for a deeper awareness of the presence of his Emmanuel, God-with-us, in your daily life.

Fourth Sunday of Advent Countdown to Christmas: Eight

O Leader of the House of Israel,
giver of the Law of Moses on Sinai:
come to rescue us with your mighty power!

Preparation: *Come, Holy Spirit, enlighten the eyes of my heart.* Be present to the God who is always present to you. Call to mind his loving care for you and spend the first minute of your prayer just resting in the free, unearned gift of loving and being loved. Let gratitude rise in your heart.

Set the Scene: Ask God for a deeper awareness of the presence of his Emmanuel, God-with-us, in your daily life. The betrothal of Mary and Joseph was a legal marriage. In accordance with the traditions of the time, young people married early and then prepared to live together. Joseph would have been preparing a place for his wife at his father's house. Picture the progress of this construction project: Where was Joseph sleeping? Use your imagination to set the scene. Read through this passage slowly and prayerfully.

MATTHEW 1:18–24 (LECTIONARY)

This is how the birth of Jesus Christ came about.
When his mother Mary was betrothed to Joseph,
but before they lived together,
she was found with child through the Holy Spirit.
Joseph her husband, since he was a righteous man,
yet unwilling to expose her to shame,
decided to divorce her quietly.
Such was his intention when, behold,
the angel of the Lord appeared to him in a dream and said,

"Joseph, son of David,
do not be afraid to take Mary your wife into your home.
For it is through the Holy Spirit
that this child has been conceived in her.
She will bear a son and you are to name him Jesus,
because he will save his people from their sins."
All this took place to fulfill
what the Lord had said through the prophet:

Behold, the virgin conceive and bear a son,
and they shall name him Emmanuel,

which means "God is with us."
When Joseph awoke,
he did as the angel of the Lord had commanded him
and took his wife into his home.

Action! Adultery was not only a sin, but it was also a crime, punishable by stoning to death. "Divorcing her quietly" would mean not denouncing her as an adulteress. It would mean, in essence, that the whole town thought Joseph was a deadbeat dad who had got his wife pregnant and then refused to live with her. It was God who gave the law that put Joseph in this predicament. Yet, God will also show him a way through. God sees Joseph's willingness to sacrifice for his wife and invites him to a different form of sacrifice. What did it mean to Joseph to hear "God is with us" in his difficult situation? Read the passage again and let the scene unfold. What does Joseph experience through this dream? What does he think or feel? How does he act on the new information?

Acknowledge: When have you been called to sacrifice? When has the presence of God helped you through a difficult conundrum? Notice your strongest thought, feeling, or desire.

Relate: Speak to God about what is on your heart. Let him look at you with love. How does he respond?

Receive: Receive whatever is in God's heart for you — his thoughts, feelings, desires. Read the passage a third time.

Respond: Now answer him back again. Just be with the Lord for a minute or two before moving on.

SUGGESTIONS FOR JOURNALING
1. I found God in the midst of my struggles when ...
2. My greatest fear or struggle seems to be ...
3. I sensed God communicating to me ...
4. I feel peace when ...
5. God's love is inviting me to a new way of seeing, thinking, or acting today, as Christmas is now just one week away ...

After you've journaled, close with a brief conversation thanking God for today's prayer time. Then pray an Our Father.

December 19 — Monday
Countdown to Christmas: Seven

O Root of Jesse's stem,
sign of God's love for all his people:
come to save us without delay!

Preparation: *Come, Holy Spirit, enlighten the eyes of my heart.* Be present to the God who is always present to you. Call to mind his loving care for you and spend the first minute of your prayer just resting in the free, unearned gift of loving and being loved. Let gratitude rise in your heart.

Set the Scene: Ask God for a deeper awareness of the presence of his Emmanuel, God-with-us, in your daily life. Read the passage. As you do, set the scene in your mind. We see an old priest going about his daily duties. What does the Temple look like? What does the angel look like? Picture the people outside waiting for Zechariah to emerge from the smoky, incense-filled Temple.

LUKE 1:5–25 (LECTIONARY)
In the days of Herod, King of Judea,
there was a priest named Zechariah
of the priestly division of Abijah;
his wife was from the daughters of Aaron,
and her name was Elizabeth.
Both were righteous in the eyes of God,
observing all the commandments
and ordinances of the Lord blamelessly.
But they had no child, because Elizabeth was barren
and both were advanced in years.

Once when he was serving as priest
in his division's turn before God,

according to the practice of the priestly service,
he was chosen by lot
to enter the sanctuary of the Lord to burn incense.
Then, when the whole assembly of the people was praying
    outside
at the hour of the incense offering,
the angel of the Lord appeared to him,
standing at the right of the altar of incense.
Zechariah was troubled by what he saw, and fear came
    upon him.

But the angel said to him, "Do not be afraid, Zechariah,
because your prayer has been heard.
Your wife Elizabeth will bear you a son,
and you shall name him John.
And you will have joy and gladness,
and many will rejoice at his birth,
for he will be great in the sight of the Lord.
He will drink neither wine nor strong drink.
He will be filled with the Holy Spirit even from his mother's
    womb,
and he will turn many of the children of Israel
to the Lord their God.
He will go before him in the spirit and power of Elijah
to turn the hearts of fathers toward children
and the disobedient to the understanding of the righteous,
to prepare a people fit for the Lord."

Then Zechariah said to the angel,
"How shall I know this?
For I am an old man, and my wife is advanced in years."
And the angel said to him in reply,
"I am Gabriel, who stand before God.
I was sent to speak to you and to announce to you this
    good news.
But now you will be speechless and unable to talk

until the day these things take place,
because you did not believe my words,
which will be fulfilled at their proper time."
Meanwhile the people were waiting for Zechariah
and were amazed that he stayed so long in the sanctuary.
But when he came out, he was unable to speak to them,
and they realized that he had seen a vision in the sanctu-
ary. He was gesturing to them but remained mute.

Then, when his days of ministry were completed, he went
home.

After this time his wife Elizabeth conceived,
and she went into seclusion for five months, saying,
"So has the Lord done for me at a time when he has seen fit
to take away my disgrace before others."

Action! Today's antiphon is drawn from Isaiah 11:1–10. King David's line had long ago been "cut off" from royal power. But God would be raising up a new shoot from the "stump of Jesse" (King David's father), and "his dwellings shall be glorious." In a similar way, Zechariah and Elizabeth have long given up the dream of having their own child. Even though Zechariah is ministering in the Temple, the last thing he expects is for an angel to emerge from the clouds of incense. What does he think or feel when the angel unexpectedly appears to him? How does he feel when he walks out of the Temple? How does Elizabeth feel? Read the passage a second time and use your imagination. Notice what stands out to you.

Acknowledge: Even though you are praying, and have connected with God in the past, do you doubt that God is present or will speak to you in a way you can understand? Is there a particular word, phrase, or moment that jumps out at you from this reading? What thoughts or feelings are stirred up by this reading? What is the desire of your heart?

Relate: Speak to God about the desires of your heart. Do you believe he is listening and will answer your prayers? Let him look at you with love.

How does he respond?

Receive: Read the passage a third time, or just the part that spoke to you. Open your heart to believe in God's presence with you and to receive whatever is in God's heart for you — his thoughts, feelings, desires, his Good News for you. Do you believe that God can, and will, do good things in your life?

Respond: Continue the conversation. Enjoy God's loving presence with you in your current place of prayer before moving on.

SUGGESTIONS FOR JOURNALING

1. The thing that spoke to me most was …
2. I felt God stirring up a desire for …
3. I have a hard time trusting when …
4. My greatest fear or struggle seems to be …
5. I sensed God was with me and wanted me to know …

After you've journaled, close with a brief conversation giving thanks to God for being with you in your prayer today. Then pray an Our Father.

December 20 — Tuesday
Countdown to Christmas: Six

O Key of David,
opening the gates of God's eternal Kingdom:
come and free the prisoners of darkness!

Preparation: *Come, Holy Spirit, enlighten the eyes of my heart.* Be present to the God who is always present to you. Call to mind his loving care for you and spend the first minute of your prayer just resting in the free, unearned gift of loving and being loved. Let gratitude rise in your heart.

Set the Scene: Ask God for the grace of his loving presence with you, Emmanuel, to break into your daily life and take root in your heart. Read the passage through. Tradition usually sets the Annunciation at Mary's home in Nazareth. What time of day was it? Perhaps Mary has paused from her chores for a little prayer time. Use your imagination to set the scene.

LUKE 1:26–38 (LECTIONARY)
In the sixth month,
the angel Gabriel was sent from God
to a town of Galilee called Nazareth,
to a virgin betrothed to a man named Joseph,
of the house of David,
and the virgin's name was Mary.
And coming to her, he said,
"Hail, full of grace! The Lord is with you."
But she was greatly troubled at what was said
and pondered what sort of greeting this might be.
Then the angel said to her,
"Do not be afraid, Mary,
for you have found favor with God.

Behold, you will conceive in your womb and bear a son,
and you shall name him Jesus.
He will be great and will be called Son of the Most High,
and the Lord God will give him the throne of David his
*   father,*
and he will rule over the house of Jacob forever,
and of his Kingdom there will be no end."

But Mary said to the angel,
"How can this be,
since I have no relations with a man?"
And the angel said to her in reply,
"The Holy Spirit will come upon you,
and the power of the Most High will overshadow you.
Therefore the child to be born
will be called holy, the Son of God.
And behold, Elizabeth, your relative,
has also conceived a son in her old age,
and this is the sixth month for her who was called barren;
for nothing will be impossible for God."

Mary said, "Behold, I am the handmaid of the Lord.
May it be done to me according to your word."
Then the angel departed from her.

Action! Play the scene forward in your mind. Today's O Antiphon takes the key of David (see Is 22:22) in two different directions: It will open the kingdom of heaven that was closed by the sin of Adam and Eve, and it will unlock the prisoners who have been kept in darkness by that same sin. But the key doesn't have the power to unlock Mary's womb; only she can do that. All of creation, groaning under the sentence of sin, awaits her answer with bated breath. What will she say? Will we finally have the long-awaited Savior that God has promised us? Read the passage a second time.

Acknowledge: Why is this virgin greatly troubled at the angel's words?

What is in her heart at this moment? What does her "Yes" feel like for her? Notice what is going on inside of you. Do you sometimes have a hard time accepting God's plans for your life? Is God waiting for you to "unlock" your heart to him?

Relate: Speak to Mary about your thoughts and feelings. Together with her, turn to God in prayer. Share what is on your heart with complete honesty. Question God, as Mary questioned the angel. Don't hide your feelings from God.

Receive: Receive whatever is in God's heart for you — his thoughts, feelings, desires. He did all this for you. What more does he want to give you? If you have a hard time receiving, ask Mary to show you how to receive. Read the passage a third time, or just the part that speaks to you.

Respond: God wants to dwell in your heart as he dwelt in the womb of Mary. Cherish the gift of God's love, not only for you and with you, but even within you. Converse with God in your heart. Then just be with the Lord and with Mary for a minute or two before moving on.

SUGGESTIONS FOR JOURNALING

1. My heart is troubled by ...
2. How have I responded when God's plans interrupted my plans?
3. God's presence feels like ...
4. I sensed God was with me and wanted me to know ...
5. I ended prayer wanting ...

_____

_____

_____

_____

_____

_____

_____

_____

_____

_____

_____

_____

_____

_____

_____

_____

_____

_____

_____

_____

_____

_____

After you've journaled, close with a brief conversation with God giving thanks for your prayer experience. Then pray a Hail Mary.

December 21 — Wednesday
Countdown to Christmas: Five

O Emmanuel, our King and Giver of Law:
come to save us, Lord our God!

Preparation: *Come, Holy Spirit, enlighten the eyes of my heart.* Be present to the God who is always present to you. Call to mind his loving care for you and spend the first minute of your prayer just resting in the free, unearned gift of loving and being loved. Let gratitude rise in your heart.

Set the Scene: Ask for the grace to welcome Mary, the God-bearer, that your heart might leap for joy at the nearness of the promised Messiah, Emmanuel. Read the passage through and picture the scene. Tradition identifies this location as a town called Ein Karem, a hill town about five miles to the west of Jerusalem and about ninety miles from Nazareth. Elizabeth is already six months pregnant. Mary hasn't started to show yet.

LUKE 1:39–45 (LECTIONARY)
Mary set out in those days
and traveled to the hill country in haste
to a town of Judah,
where she entered the house of Zechariah
and greeted Elizabeth.
When Elizabeth heard Mary's greeting,
the infant leaped in her womb,
and Elizabeth, filled with the Holy Spirit,
cried out in a loud voice and said,
"Most blessed are you among women,
and blessed is the fruit of your womb.
And how does this happen to me,
that the mother of my Lord should come to me?
For at the moment the sound of your greeting reached my

> *ears,*
> *the infant in my womb leaped for joy.*
> *Blessed are you who believed*
> *that what was spoken to you by the Lord*
> *would be fulfilled."*

Action! "Emmanuel" means "God-with-us" (Is 7:14). How was God with Mary on her journey to visit Elizabeth? How does Elizabeth feel in the presence of her infant Lord? How is God with you right now? Read the passage a second time.

Acknowledge: Christmas is a busy time for visiting and receiving visitors. Do your visitors bring the presence of Jesus to your home, or do they bring worries of being judged for a messy home? When you visit others, how do you bring Jesus with you to their home? When did you leap for joy at God's presence in your life?

Relate: Let your thoughts and feelings rise to the surface. Speak to God what is in your heart.

Receive: How does God the Father view this scene? How does he gaze upon your visits and visitors? Receive whatever is in God's heart for you — his thoughts, feelings, desires. Read the passage a third time.

Respond: Converse with God in your heart. Then just savor the presence of Jesus for a minute or two before moving on.

SUGGESTIONS FOR JOURNALING
1. My heart leaped for joy when …
2. I sensed God saying to me …
3. I ended prayer wanting …
4. Is there a way I can "go in haste" to share with another the joy I am receiving through these Advent prayer times?

After you've journaled, close with a brief conversation with God giving thanks for your prayer experience. Then pray a Hail Mary.

December 22 — Thursday
Countdown to Christmas: Four

O King of all nations and keystone of the Church:
come and save man, whom you formed from the dust!

Preparation: *Come, Holy Spirit, enlighten the eyes of my heart.* Be present to the God who is always present to you. Call to mind his loving care for you and spend the first minute of your prayer just resting in the free, unearned gift of loving and being loved. Let gratitude rise in your heart.

Lectio: Ask in your own words that God might fill your heart with the joy of Emmanuel, God-with-us. Read the passage slowly and prayerfully. This Scripture is called the *Magnificat* (which is the first word of this passage in Latin). It is a hymn of praise to God who has been faithful to his promises from Abraham until today. This could very well be a song that the saints sing in heaven. Is there one word or phrase that you feel moved to focus on?

LUKE 1:46–56 (LECTIONARY)
Mary said:

> "My soul proclaims the greatness of the Lord;
>   my spirit rejoices in God my savior.
>   for he has looked upon his lowly servant.
> From this day all generations will call me blessed.
>   the Almighty has done great things for me,
>   and holy is his Name.
>   He has mercy on those who fear him
>   in every generation.
> He has shown the strength of his arm,
>   and has scattered the proud in their conceit.

133

He has cast down the mighty from their thrones
and has lifted up the lowly.
He has filled the hungry with good things,
and the rich he has sent away empty.
He has come to the help of his servant Israel
for he remembered his promise of mercy,
the promise he made to our fathers,
to Abraham and his children forever."

Mary remained with Elizabeth about three months
and then returned to her home.

Meditatio: Have you noticed recent news stories where God was humbling the proud or lifting up the lowly? How has God done great things for you? Have you experienced his mercy, blessing, or strength? Or perhaps you feel lowly, humbled, someone who needs to be raised from the dust, and you are waiting for the king of all nations to come rescue you with the might of his arm. Reflect for a few minutes, or just focus on the word or phrase that speaks to you. Then read the passage again slowly.

Oratio: Speak to God what is on your heart and mind, your thoughts, feelings, and desires. When you are done speaking, read the passage one more time.

Contemplatio: Open your heart to receive what God wants to give you. Maybe it is a thought, a word, or a sense of peace. God is with you in this ordinary moment. Even his challenging words come with love. Rest in and savor his love for you. Be present. Be lowly.

SUGGESTIONS FOR JOURNALING
1. My favorite word or phrase was …
2. God fulfilled his promises to me when …
3. I rejoice in God my savior when I recall …
4. The people and the world around me most need to hear …
5. Mary takes Jesus with her wherever she goes. How can I take Jesus with me on my journey today?

_____

_____

_____

_____

_____

_____

_____

_____

_____

_____

_____

_____

_____

_____

_____

_____

_____

_____

_____

_____

_____

After you've journaled, close with a brief conversation with God giving thanks for your prayer experience. Then close by reading today's Scripture one more time as a prayer of praise and thanksgiving.

December 23 — Friday
Countdown to Christmas: Three

O King of all nations and keystone of the Church:
come and save man, whom you formed from the dust!

Preparation: *Come, Holy Spirit, enlighten the eyes of my heart.* Be present to the God who is always present to you. Call to mind his loving care for you and spend the first minute of your prayer just resting in the free, unearned gift of loving and being loved. Let gratitude rise in your heart.

Set the Scene: Ask God for the grace to see Emmanuel, God-with-us, in the lives of your friends and relatives. It's easy to imagine Elizabeth's neighbors and relatives gathering around to celebrate the birth of a healthy baby boy. The circumcision was like a baptism party. The name John means "God is gracious." Set the scene in your imagination. Populate it with villagers.

LUKE 1:57–66 (LECTIONARY)

When the time arrived for Elizabeth to have her child
she gave birth to a son.
Her neighbors and relatives heard
that the Lord had shown his great mercy toward her,
and they rejoiced with her.
When they came on the eighth day to circumcise the
child,
they were going to call him Zechariah after his father,
but his mother said in reply,
"No. He will be called John."
But they answered her,
"There is no one among your relatives who has this name."
So they made signs, asking his father what he wished him to
be called.

He asked for a tablet and wrote, "John is his name,"
and all were amazed.
Immediately his mouth was opened, his tongue freed,
and he spoke blessing God.
Then fear came upon all their neighbors,
*   and all these matters were discussed*
throughout the hill country of Judea.
All who heard these things took them to heart, saying,
"What, then, will this child be?
For surely the hand of the Lord was with him."

Action! Read the passage a second time and play the scene forward in your mind. See the looks on the faces of the guests and their excited conversation. Zechariah is only a silent participant — imagine the look on his face as he meets his son and welcomes his guests. Imagine the look on everyone's face when suddenly he can speak again! Even though Mary isn't mentioned, she was probably in the crowd somewhere — why else would she have remained for three months with Elizabeth? Place yourself within the crowd.

Acknowledge: Read the antiphon for today. How do you feel at the birth of this child who will prepare the way for the *king of all nations and keystone of the Church*? What thoughts and feelings rise in your heart?

Relate: Speak to God what is in your heart. If you have a hard time expressing yourself, maybe Zechariah can help.

Receive: Read the passage a third time and receive whatever is in God's heart for you — his thoughts, feelings, desires. Does your heavenly Father look at you like Zechariah looked at his son, John?

Respond: Let the Father look at you and look back at him. Just savor the joy of being your Father's child for a few minutes before moving on.

SUGGESTIONS FOR JOURNALING
1. I was surprised by …

2. Zechariah teaches me …
3. The Father seemed to be saying to me …
4. When do I feel tongue-tied, or when do I find it hard to speak to God? Or was there something today that I had a hard time receiving and accepting?
5. I ended prayer wanting …

After you've journaled, close with a brief conversation with God giving thanks for your prayer experience. Then pray an Our Father.

December 24 — Saturday
Countdown to Christmas: Two

O Radiant Dawn, splendor of eternal light, sun of justice:
come and shine on those who dwell in darkness
and in the shadow of death.

Preparation: *Come, Holy Spirit, enlighten the eyes of my heart.* Be present to the God who is always present to you. Call to mind his loving care for you and spend the first minute of your prayer just resting in the free, unearned gift of loving and being loved. Let gratitude rise in your heart.

Lectio: Ask for the grace to see Emmanuel, God-with-us, in your own history and in the present moment. Zechariah hasn't spoken for nine months — and now he has a lot to say! He proclaims that this child will brighten all the world and bring a freedom far greater than the Israelites experienced as they left Egypt. Read this passage slowly and prayerfully. Is there a word or phrase that speaks to you most strongly?

LUKE 1:67–79 (LECTIONARY)

Zechariah his father, filled with the Holy Spirit,
*   prophesied, saying:*

> *"Blessed be the Lord, the God of Israel;*
> *   for he has come to his people and set them free.*
> *He has raised up for us a mighty Savior,*
> *   born of the house of his servant David.*
> *Through his prophets he promised of old*
> *   that he would save us from our enemies,*
> *   from the hands of all who hate us.*
> *He promised to show mercy to our fathers*
> *   and to remember his holy covenant.*
> *This was the oath he swore to our father Abraham:*

> *to set us free from the hand of our enemies,*
> *free to worship him without fear,*
> *holy and righteous in his sight*
>   *all the days of our life.*
> *You, my child, shall be called the prophet of the Most High,*
>   *for you will go before the Lord to prepare his way,*
>   *to give his people knowledge of salvation*
>   *by the forgiveness of their sins.*
> *In the tender compassion of our God*
>   *the dawn from on high shall break upon us,*
>   *to shine on those who dwell in darkness and the*
>   *shadow of death,*
>   *and to guide our feet into the way of peace."*

Meditatio: *O Radiant Dawn!* The dawn from on high that shall break upon us. You guessed it, that is the word *Oriens*. With this being the day before Christmas, it is as though the dawn is just starting to peek out over the hills. Have you felt God's light shining more brightly these last twenty-seven days? Has God been guiding your feet into the way of peace? Read the passage again, or maybe just the part that speaks to you.

Oratio: What do you want to say to God, with the birth of his Son so close at hand? Speak to God what is on your heart and mind. When you are done speaking, soak in the passage.

Contemplatio: Read the passage one more time. Open your heart to receive what God wants to give you. God loves every child like an only child. Rest in and savor his love for you. Let the dawn from on high shine upon you. Bask in the light of God's love for a few minutes before moving on.

SUGGESTIONS FOR JOURNALING

1. God has set me free from …
2. I experienced the forgiveness of sins in a personal way when …

3. I feel the light of God shining in my heart when …
4. God's love feels like …
5. I need patience as I wait for …

_____

_____

_____

_____

_____

_____

_____

_____

_____

_____

_____

_____

_____

_____

_____

_____

_____

_____

REVIEW

If you have time, go back and review the previous week. Here are some questions that might help you.

1. Where did I notice God, and what was he doing or saying?
2. How has the countdown made Christmas Day a richer experience for me?
3. What was the biggest grace or gift I received from God on this pilgrim journey?
4. I'm grateful for …
5. I was most able to rest in God's love for me when …
6. It turns out what I really wanted for Christmas was …

_____

_____

_____

_____

_____

_____

_____

_____

_____

_____

_____

_____

_____

_____

_____

_____

Conclude by conversing with God about your review. **Acknowledge** what you have been experiencing. **Relate** it to him. **Receive** what he wants to give you. **Respond** to him. Then savor that image of God's loving presence and rest there for a minute or two. Then read today's Scripture one more time as a prayer of praise and thanksgiving.

Week Five

A Feast Fit for a King

The feast of Christmas is too big to fit into one day. For eight days we celebrate the long-awaited radiant Dawn, the Sun of Justice and King all nations who is Christ the Lord. I tell schoolchildren that the Octave of Christmas means you have to eat Christmas treats every day for eight days. The Gloria is sung at Mass for all eight days of the octave. Several of these days are special feast days dedicated to particular saints.

During the octave, swap out the purple and pink candles on your Advent wreath for white candles. Light them when you eat your family meals and sing a Christmas carol together each time. And keep making time for your pilgrimage! We've come through Advent and have only begun to journey through Christmas.

Grace of the Week: As we celebrate Christmas and the octave, our readings will be drawn from the lectionary's readings for each feast or for the daily Mass readings. Ask God for a deeper sense of peace and joy in the birth of Jesus, and pray that his love will fill your heart with warmth and light.

The text below, taken from the Roman Martyrology, presents the birth of Jesus as one would announce the birth of a king or emperor. The announcement is recited or chanted on December 24, during the celebration of the Liturgy of the Hours or before the Christmas Mass during the Night.

ANNOUNCEMENT OF THE BIRTH OF CHRIST FROM THE ROMAN MARTYROLOGY

The Twenty-fifth Day of December, when ages beyond number had run their course from the creation of the world, when God in the beginning created heaven and earth, and formed man in his own likeness;

when century upon century had passed since the Almighty set his bow in the clouds after the Great Flood, as a sign of covenant and peace; in the twenty-first century since Abraham, our

149

father in faith, came out of Ur of the Chaldees;

in the thirteenth century since the People of Israel were led by Moses in the Exodus from Egypt; around the thousandth year since David was anointed King;

in the sixty-fifth week of the prophecy of Daniel; in the one hundred and ninety-fourth Olympiad; in the year seven hundred and fifty-two since the foundation of the City of Rome; in the forty-second year of the reign of Caesar Octavian Augustus, the whole world being at peace,

Jesus Christ, eternal God and Son of the eternal Father, desiring to consecrate the world by his most loving presence, was conceived by the Holy Spirit, and when nine months had passed since his conception, was born of the Virgin Mary in Bethlehem of Judah, and was made man:

The Nativity of Our Lord Jesus Christ according to the flesh.
—Appendix 1 of the Roman Missal, Third Edition

December 25 — Sunday

The Nativity of Our Lord Jesus Christ

Preparation: *Come, Holy Spirit, enlighten the eyes of my heart.* Be present to the God who is always present to you. Call to mind his loving care for you and spend the first minute of your prayer just resting in the free, unearned gift of loving and being loved. Let gratitude rise in your heart.

Set the Scene: Ask God for a deeper sense of peace and joy in the birth of Jesus, and pray that his love will fill your heart with warmth and light. We like to think of the Nativity as something easy, peaceful, and cozy. But our Gospel implies crowds thronging to fulfill Caesar's decree, a long journey on dusty roads with a very pregnant woman, and the Holy Family finding themselves homeless at the most inopportune time. Read through the Gospel to set the scene in your imagination.

LUKE 2:1–14 MASS AT MIDNIGHT (LECTIONARY)
LUKE 2:15–20 MASS AT DAWN (LECTIONARY)

*In those days a decree went out from Caesar Augustus
that the whole world should be enrolled.
This was the first enrollment,
when Quirinius was governor of Syria.
So all went to be enrolled, each to his own town.
And Joseph too went up from Galilee from the town of
    Nazareth
to Judea, to the city of David that is called Bethlehem,
because he was of the house and family of David,
to be enrolled with Mary, his betrothed, who was with
    child.
While they were there,
the time came for her to have her child,
and she gave birth to her firstborn son.*

She wrapped him in swaddling clothes and laid him in a
    manger,
because there was no room for them in the inn.

Now there were shepherds in that region living in the fields
and keeping the night watch over their flock.
The angel of the Lord appeared to them
and the glory of the Lord shone around them,
and they were struck with great fear.
The angel said to them,
"Do not be afraid;
for behold, I proclaim to you good news of great joy
that will be for all the people.
For today in the city of David
a savior has been born for you who is Christ and Lord.
And this will be a sign for you:
you will find an infant wrapped in swaddling clothes
and lying in a manger."
And suddenly there was a multitude of the heavenly host
with the angel,
praising God and saying:
    "Glory to God in the highest
        and on earth peace to those on whom his favor rests."
When the angels went away from them to heaven,
the shepherds said to one another,
"Let us go, then, to Bethlehem
to see this thing that has taken place,
which the Lord has made known to us."
So they went in haste and found Mary and Joseph,
and the infant lying in the manger.
When they saw this,
they made known the message
that had been told them about this child.
All who heard it were amazed
by what had been told them by the shepherds.
And Mary kept all these things,

reflecting on them in her heart.
Then the shepherds returned,
glorifying and praising God
for all they had heard and seen,
just as it had been told to them.

Action! Sometimes we find ourselves trying to make a life for ourselves as world events swirl around us. Did Joseph and Mary know why they were making this journey? Did they perhaps fret about the destination and the challenge of finding housing? God provides an unorthodox, but effective, bed for his little Son. God "lifts up the lowly" by inviting humble shepherds to come and adore the newborn king. Where do you find yourself in this scene? Read the passage a second time and play the scene forward in your mind.

Acknowledge: You are watching God fulfill his promise of mercy. What is in Mary's heart? Joseph's heart? The heart of the shepherds? Your heart?

Relate: Perhaps you can ask Mary to let you hold her child. What do you feel in your heart as you contemplate the Savior? Speak to God what is in your heart.

Receive: Receive whatever is in God's heart for you. Read the passage a third time.

Respond: Just savor the joy of holding the Son and being held by the Father for a little while. Let God the Father gaze at you as you gaze on the face of his Son.

SUGGESTIONS FOR JOURNALING

1. The glory of the Lord shone in my Christmas celebration when ...
2. I felt God's love most strongly ...
3. What does it mean to say that the prophecies were meant for me, the Messiah was prepared for me, that Jesus was born for me?

4. The Father seemed to be saying to me …
5. I was surprised by …
6. My heart rested when …

Spend a minute thanking Jesus for being God-with-you in your prayer experience today, then close with an Our Father.

December 26 — Monday
Second Day in the Octave of Christmas

SAINT STEPHEN, DEACON AND MARTYR

Stephen was one of seven men chosen to be the first deacons of the infant church (see Acts 6:1–6). They were ordained specifically to take over the Church's care for the widows, a sign that charity for the needy is an essential part of the Gospel. He did great wonders and signs and preached the Gospel with so much wisdom that his opponents were confounded. They falsely accused him of blasphemy, and a mob stoned him to death (Acts 6:8—8:1). He is the first in a long line of faithful servants who gave their lives in witness to the true King. This feast reminds us that Jesus was born into time so that Stephen, and all of us, could be born into eternity.

Preparation: *Come, Holy Spirit, enlighten the eyes of my heart.* Be present to the God who is always present to you. Call to mind his loving care for you and spend the first minute of your prayer just resting in the free, unearned gift of loving and being loved. Let gratitude rise in your heart.

Set the Scene: Ask God for a deeper sense of peace and joy in the birth of Jesus, and pray that his love will fill your heart with warmth and light. Hopefully we are still glowing with the light of the Nativity scene. We want the peace and joy of baby Jesus to enter more deeply into our hearts. The Church has long celebrated the feast of the first martyr the day after the birthday of Jesus. Whenever the Church gives us something incongruous, such as a mob murdering an innocent man, it can be a chance to find deeper meaning and new connections within our faith. The young Christian Church has been spreading rapidly. Stephen is an effective apologist, meaning that he explains or defends the truths of the Faith. He is also filled with the Holy Spirit; the "signs and wonders" the Bible mentions him working are most likely miracles of healing and exorcism. His opponents try to prove him wrong through philosophical and theological debates, but the debate only proves him more right. They resort to violence. Read the passage and notice your own feelings as you read it.

ACTS 6:8–10; 7:54–59 (LECTIONARY)

Stephen, filled with grace and power,
was working great wonders and signs among the people.
Certain members of the so-called Synagogue of Freedmen,
Cyrenians, and Alexandrians,
and people from Cilicia and Asia,
came forward and debated with Stephen,
but they could not withstand the wisdom and the spirit
with which he spoke.

When they heard this, they were infuriated,
and they ground their teeth at him.
But he, filled with the Holy Spirit,
looked up intently to heaven
and saw the glory of God and Jesus standing at the right
hand of God,
and he said,
"Behold, I see the heavens opened and the Son of Man
standing at the right hand of God."
But they cried out in a loud voice, covered their ears,
and rushed upon him together.
They threw him out of the city, and began to stone him.
The witnesses laid down their cloaks
at the feet of a young man named Saul.
As they were stoning Stephen, he called out,
"Lord Jesus, receive my spirit."

Action! As the whirlwind of anger and hatred unfolds around him, focus on the peace in Stephen's heart. Acts 6:15 says, "All those who sat in the Sanhedrin looked intently at him and saw that his face was like the face of an angel." The heavens are opened, and Stephen sees Jesus himself in glory. He ends his life in imitation of Jesus' death on the cross. Like Jesus' own death, the death of Stephen is a story of redemption. The Saul who appears at the end of today's reading will appear again on January 25. Read the passage a second time, slowly and prayerfully.

Acknowledge: Place yourself in the scene. Focus on the part that speaks to you. How does Stephen glorify God? How does God glorify Stephen? What thoughts, feelings, and desires are rising in your heart? Does Stephen inspire you with courage to lay down your life for the Christ Child? Or does this passage make you uncomfortable?

Relate: The same Jesus who appeared to Stephen standing at the right hand of God is now standing with you. Turn to him. Share with him honestly what is on your heart, without fear of "saying the wrong thing" or being judged. Jesus already knows what you are thinking, but he's waiting for you to turn to him. Read the passage a third time, or just the part that spoke to you.

Receive: Now open your heart to how Jesus wants to respond to you — a word, a phrase, or just his silent, loving presence. Spend a few minutes in the presence of the Almighty who became a little child.

Respond: You, too, are valuable to God, as Stephen was valuable to him. Savor the light of the Holy Spirit shining on your heart and respond to whatever God is giving you. Spend a minute or two in silent conversation before moving on.

SUGGESTIONS FOR JOURNALING

1. I never realized that …
2. I see a new connection between Christmas and the feast of Stephen …
3. My strongest thought, feeling, or desire was …
4. Jesus gave me the gift of …
5. I ended prayer with a new appreciation of the Christmas story …

After you've journaled, thank God for his presence with you and his love for you in today's prayer time. Join with Stephen and all the members of God's heavenly family as you pray an Our Father.

December 27 — Tuesday
Third Day in the Octave of Christmas

SAINT JOHN, APOSTLE AND EVANGELIST

Born in Bethsaida on the Sea of Galilee, the brother of James and a fisherman by trade, John was called to follow Jesus while mending his nets (see Mk 1:19–20). Along with his brother James and fellow fisherman Peter, he was present at the Transfiguration of the Lord (Mk 9:2–8). The Gospel that bears his name refers to him only as "the beloved disciple." He was the one who reclined next to Jesus at the Last Supper (Jn 13:23) and stood at the foot of the cross as Jesus died. Jesus entrusted his mother to John's care (Jn 19:26–27). He wrote the fourth Gospel, three epistles, and is credited with the Book of Revelation. He was the only apostle not to be martyred. Tradition holds that he was miraculously preserved from attempts to kill him and died in exile on the island of Patmos.

Preparation: *Come, Holy Spirit, enlighten the eyes of my heart.* Be present to the God who is always present to you. Call to mind his loving care for you and spend the first minute of your prayer just resting in the free, unearned gift of loving and being loved. Let gratitude rise in your heart.

Set the Scene: Ask God for a deeper sense of peace and joy in the birth of Jesus, and pray that his love will fill your heart with warmth and light. We have journeyed from a cradle to a mob scene and now to a graveyard. There are places where we expect to find God's loving presence shining brightly (Christmas, church, a birthday) and places where we expect not to find God's love shining (sin, death). But the Christmas story is a story of light shining in darkness. From a stable-cave to a tomb-cave, swaddling clothes to burial cloths, shepherds to fishermen, the story of the Christ is a story of happy surprises. Be prepared to be surprised by God's loving care today.

Jesus died on Friday and was buried in a new tomb. The disciples went into hiding to escape a similar fate. Now it's early Sunday morning (the first day of the week) and the tomb is suddenly empty. Picture the rock-hewn cave with a large stone rolled away, and the dawn's light shining on the empty burial cloths. Read the passage slowly and prayerfully.

JOHN 20:1a, 2–8 (LECTIONARY)

On the first day of the week,
Mary Magdalene ran and went to Simon Peter
and to the other disciple whom Jesus loved, and told
them, "They have taken the Lord from the tomb,
and we do not know where they put him."
So Peter and the other disciple went out and came to the
    tomb.
They both ran, but the other disciple ran faster than Peter
and arrived at the tomb first;
he bent down and saw the burial cloths there, but did not
    go in.
When Simon Peter arrived after him,
he went into the tomb and saw the burial cloths there,
and the cloth that had covered his head,
not with the burial cloths but rolled up in a separate place.
Then the other disciple also went in,
the one who had arrived at the tomb first,
and he saw and believed.

Action! Multiple times in the months leading up to the crucifixion, Jesus had predicted his passion, death, and resurrection (see Mk 8:31–33; 9:30–32; 10:32–34). The disciples, however, were so focused on the idea that Jesus would be a glorious king (Mk 10:35–45) that they cannot digest his message. What is Mary Magdalene thinking and feeling? How about Peter? John? Read the Gospel a second time and notice what is going on with each character.

Acknowledge: How would you feel if, three days after Grandma's funeral, you returned to the cemetery to find her grave dug up, her casket opened, and nothing inside but the clothes she had been buried in? What does the Resurrection feel like as a present reality? Be present to the story today.

Relate: The Risen Jesus has not abandoned his disciples. In just a few more lines, he will surprise Mary Magdalene with his loving presence (see Jn 20:11–18). The Risen Jesus is with you right now. Turn to him. Share with him what is in your heart.

Receive: Read the passage a third time. What does Jesus want to share with you? Be with him and receive what is in his heart for you. Our God is a God of surprises. Allow yourself to be surprised by the peace, joy, and Good News that God wants to give you today.

Respond: Continue the conversation with him. Then just be with him for a minute or two and savor the Light who is Life and Love.

SUGGESTIONS FOR JOURNALING
1. I was surprised by …
2. I have a hard time finding God in my dark ___ (place, experience, emotion, sinful habit, etc.) …
3. I have seen God's light shining in my darkness when …
4. The presence of the Risen Jesus gives me …
5. Jesus wanted me to know, to experience, to realize that …
6. As a result of today's prayer time, I find myself more able to believe that …

After you've journaled, let the message of today's prayer experience sink into your heart and fill you with light and gratitude. Then pray an Our Father.

December 28 — Wednesday
Fourth Day in the Octave of Christmas

THE HOLY INNOCENTS, MARTYRS

Preparation: *Come Holy Spirit, enlighten the eyes of my heart.* Be present to the God who is always present to you. Call to mind his loving care for you and spend the first minute of your prayer just resting in the free, unearned gift of loving and being loved. Let gratitude rise in your heart.

Set the Scene: Ask God for a deeper sense of peace and joy in the birth of Jesus, and pray that his love will fill your heart with warmth and light. Inspired by a star, magi from the East arrive in Jerusalem looking for a newborn king of the Jews. The present king, and the Jewish people, too, fear a power struggle (see Mt 2:3). King Herod puts on a good face, politely welcomes the foreign visitors, and points them to Bethlehem as the prophesied birthplace of the Christ. He will help them find the child so they can help him kill the child. The magi, however, are warned in a dream and they take another way home (Mt 2:12). Herod responds with even greater violence.

MATTHEW 2:13–18 (LECTIONARY)

When the magi had departed, behold,
the angel of the Lord appeared to Joseph in a dream and
said, "Rise, take the child and his mother, flee to Egypt,
and stay there until I tell you.
Herod is going to search for the child to destroy him."
Joseph rose and took the child and his mother by night
and departed for Egypt.
He stayed there until the death of Herod,
that what the Lord had said through the prophet might be
*   fulfilled,*

Out of Egypt I called my son.

When Herod realized that he had been deceived by the
magi,
he became furious.
He ordered the massacre of all the boys in Bethlehem and
its vicinity
two years old and under,
in accordance with the time he had ascertained from the
magi.
Then was fulfilled what had been said through Jeremiah
the prophet:

A voice was heard in Ramah,
    sobbing and loud lamentation;
Rachel weeping for her children,
    and she would not be consoled,
since they were no more.

Action! The Bible does not shrink from describing human depravity. We are meant to see in this dark and disturbing passage echoes of Pharaoh killing the male children of the Hebrew slaves (see Ex 1:15–22) and God saving Moses so that he could save his people (Ex 2). Jesus will not escape forever; one day he will return to die for Herod's sins and your sins. Picture the Holy Family sneaking out of Bethlehem as the royal guards march in. Focus on Joseph, Mary, and the baby Jesus as they flee toward Egypt. What do they think, feel, and experience? How is God with them on their journey?

Acknowledge: What thoughts and feelings do you experience as you read this passage? Is there an episode from your own life that allows you to relate to the pain of these mothers? Or are there disturbing news stories that remind you of this episode from the Bible? Take a moment to listen to your heart and let any pain, confusion, or anger rise to the surface.

Relate: Just as the Bible does not shy away from human depravity, so God is not afraid of your pain, hurt, or anger. Speak to him honestly. Rage at him if you need to.

Receive: Now focus on God and his loving presence. Realize that Mary and Joseph also suffered from this experience. They became refugees in a foreign land and left behind the life they had known. But God was with them in the Christ Child. How is God with you in your pain? How is God with suffering humanity today? Where do you see his light shining in the darkness of sin and death? Be open to receiving whatever he wants to give you or show you. If you feel stuck, ask Mary and Joseph to help you.

Respond: Read the passage a third time. Let God's light shine on you. Bask in his loving care for you and for each and every human being. See God holding every mother who has lost a child. Hold the Christ Child and let him hold you. Bask in God's loving care for you for a few minutes before moving on.

SUGGESTIONS FOR JOURNALING

1. How is God's light shining in the midst of my darkness?
2. How have I personally experienced darkness, confusion, or what seemed like unimaginable suffering?
3. What new way of thinking or responding am I being invited to?
4. How is God calling me out of darkness like Joseph was called out of darkness?
5. How am I called to shine the light of God's loving care on some person or situation that is close to me?

After you've journaled, thank God for the experience of his loving care today, then pray an Our Father.

December 29 — Thursday
Fifth Day in the Octave of Christmas

SAINT THOMAS BECKET, BISHOP AND MARTYR

Thomas Becket was born in London in 1118. Though a cleric of the diocese of Canterbury, he became chancellor to King Henry II and took a leading part in a military expedition against the French. When the archbishop died, Thomas was chosen as his replacement. Perhaps Henry wanted "his man" to be chief cleric in England. However, Thomas took his new responsibilities very seriously and began a life of penance and simplicity. He led a protracted defense of the Church's independence from the crown, which resulted in six years of exile. On this day in 1170, knights and a band of armed men slew him in his church. King Henry did public penance for this crime.

Preparation: *Come, Holy Spirit, enlighten the eyes of my heart.* Be present to the God who is always present to you. Call to mind his loving care for you and spend the first minute of your prayer just resting in the free, unearned gift of loving and being loved. Let gratitude rise in your heart.

Lectio: Ask God for a deeper sense of peace and joy in the birth of Jesus, and pray that his love will fill your heart with warmth and light. We will take a break from human depravity to focus on divine goodness. The ancients saw the order, perfection, and dependability of the heavens as a sign of what God was like. We tend to blame God for the evil in the world. Some people have a hard time even believing in a good God because of the existence of evil. However, Scripture makes it clear that evil arises from the heart of man when he is tricked by the world, the flesh, and the Devil. God himself is good and the source of all goodness. Let us praise God for his goodness, justice, and constancy. Perhaps use your imagination to picture the heavenly cosmos as you read this passage.

PSALM 96:1–2A, 2B–3, 5B–6, 7–8A, 8B–9, 10, 11–12, 13 (LECTIONARY — DECEMBER 29, 30, 31)

Sing to the LORD a new song;
   sing to the LORD, all you lands.
Sing to the LORD, bless his name;
Announce his salvation, day after day.
Tell his glory among the nations;
   among all peoples, his wondrous deeds.
The LORD made the heavens.
Splendor and majesty go before him;
   power and grandeur are in his sanctuary.
Give to the LORD, you families of nations,
   give to the LORD glory and praise;
   give to the LORD the glory due his name!
Bring gifts, and enter his courts;
   worship the LORD in holy attire.
Tremble before him, all the earth.
Say among the nations: The LORD is king.
He has made the world firm, not to be moved;
   he governs the peoples with equity.
Let the heavens be glad and the earth rejoice;
   let the sea and what fills it resound;
   let the plains be joyful and all that is in them!
Then let all the trees of the forest exult before the LORD.
The LORD comes,
   he comes to govern the earth.
He shall rule the world with justice
   and the peoples with his constancy.

Meditatio: Man is a steward of God's creation, but his stewardship will not last forever. God himself will one day return to cast out evil and darkness and to rule the world with justice and equity. The earth and all creation are excited for this moment. How have you experienced God's goodness in your own life? How have you experienced God's goodness through your *Oriens* pilgrimage this year? Reflect on your experiences, and then read the passage a second time, slowly and prayerfully.

Oratio: Saint Paul says, "We know that the whole creation is groaning in labor pains until now; and not only that, but we ourselves, who have the firstfruits of the Spirit, we also groan within ourselves as we wait for adoption, the redemption of our bodies" (Rom 8:22–23). The Lord will come to rule the earth. His Second Coming is already near. Do you tremble with excitement, or with fear? Where in your life, or in your world, are you groaning as you wait to experience God's justice and equity? Speak to God about these places that need his loving touch.

Contemplatio: Read the passage a third time, slowly and prayerfully. As you do, receive God's response to your words. What is in God's heart for you? What does God long to give you? How will he make things right for you? Rejoice that he hears you, and then spend a few minutes in prayerful communion with God before moving on.

SUGGESTIONS FOR JOURNALING

1. Gazing at the heavens, the sea, the plains, and the trees, I am reminded that …
2. The word or phrase that most spoke to me today was …
3. What am I groaning for?
4. What is God desiring to give me? What is he waiting for?
5. I ended prayer with a deeper sense that …

After you've journaled, spend a moment thanking God for his constancy in your life, then end with an Our Father.

December 30 — Friday
The Holy Family of Jesus, Mary, and Joseph

Preparation: *Come, Holy Spirit, enlighten the eyes of my heart.* Be present to the God who is always present to you. Call to mind his loving care for you and spend the first minute of your prayer just resting in the free, unearned gift of loving and being loved. Let gratitude rise in your heart.

Set the Scene: Ask God for a deeper sense of joy and peace in the birth of Jesus, that his light will shine in the dark corners of your heart and your world. This feast day is celebrated on the Sunday between Christmas and New Year's. However, in the years when there is no Sunday within the octave, the feast of the Holy Family is celebrated on December 30. That makes this year's feast day something of a refugee, displaced from its proper and dignified home on Sunday to a lesser day of the week. This was also the experience of the Holy Family as they fled from Herod into Egypt, then returned to a different town. Picture the scene in your mind as you read the passage.

MATTHEW 2:13–15, 19–23 (LECTIONARY)
When the magi had departed, behold,
the angel of the Lord appeared to Joseph in a dream and
said, "Rise, take the child and his mother, flee to Egypt,
and stay there until I tell you.
Herod is going to search for the child to destroy him."
Joseph rose and took the child and his mother by night
and departed for Egypt.
He stayed there until the death of Herod,
that what the Lord had said through the prophet might
be fulfilled,
Out of Egypt I called my son.

When Herod had died, behold,

the angel of the Lord appeared in a dream
to Joseph in Egypt and said,
"Rise, take the child and his mother and go to the land of
     Israel,
for those who sought the child's life are dead."
He rose, took the child and his mother,
and went to the land of Israel.
But when he heard that Archelaus was ruling over Judea
in place of his father Herod,
he was afraid to go back there.
And because he had been warned in a dream,
he departed for the region of Galilee.
He went and dwelt in a town called Nazareth,
so that what had been spoken through the prophets
might be fulfilled,
He shall be called a Nazorean.

Action! In the early days of the Jewish people, Egypt was a superpower. Guided by Joseph's dreams, Israel and his sons found refuge there from a famine (see Gn 46). Egypt then enslaved the Jewish people and became a symbol for the powers of the world that oppose and persecute God's children. In Jesus' day, Egypt and Israel were at peace with each other as they were both dominated by Rome. A thriving community of ex-pat Jews would have made it an attractive locale to escape from the clutches of King Herod. Read the passage again. Picture Joseph's unquestioning, prompt obedience to God's messages. What was Egypt like? What was Nazareth like? Use your imagination.

Acknowledge: My family moved a number of times as I was growing up. Being uprooted and replanted was sometimes a traumatic experience. However, I believe these moves were, in fact, orchestrated by God's hand. There were always blessings waiting for us that we would not have experienced had we stayed put. God used those experiences to help shape the person I am today. What experiences from your life connect with the experience of the Holy Family? How has God turned difficulties and even traumas into blessings in your life? Notice what stirs inside of you.

Relate: Joseph is worried for the family's safety when he finds that Herod's son is now sitting on his father's throne. He trusts in God and discovers that God shares his concerns and has an answer for him. Share your concerns with God. Be open and honest about what has been stirred up within you.

Receive: Do you have a sense of how God receives what you have shared with him? Do you have a sense of how God responds to your concerns? Sometimes you will notice an immediate response such as a word, Scripture passage, or song lyrics that come to mind. Other times you will receive a sense of peace, that God hears you and values what you have to say. Perhaps the response will come later in the form of a message from a friend or even a dream (this last option is possible, but unlikely). God doesn't stop talking just because our prayer time is over. But be open to receive whatever he wants to give you in this moment. Read the passage a third time.

Respond: Have a conversation with God or thank him for whatever it is you have received through this prayer time. Savor his loving presence with you for a few minutes before moving on.

SUGGESTIONS FOR JOURNALING

1. The Holy Family's experience resonated with my experience of …
2. I felt God calling me and guiding me when …
3. My strongest thought, feeling, or desire was …
4. I sensed that God wanted me to know …
5. I feel called to a new way of thinking, living, or acting …

After you've journaled, spend a final minute thanking God for his presence in today's prayer experience, then pray an Our Father.

December 31 — Saturday
Seventh Day in the Octave of Christmas

REVIEW

Preparation: *Come, Holy Spirit, enlighten the eyes of my heart.* Call to mind God's loving care for you and spend the first minute of your prayer just resting in the free, unearned gift of loving and being loved. Let gratitude rise in your heart.

Glance through the past week, starting with Christmas Day. What grace and blessings have you received during the Christmas Octave? Here are some questions to help you:

1. Where did I notice God, and what was he doing or saying?
2. How did I respond to what God was doing?
3. I felt God's love most strongly when …
4. I found myself struggling with …
5. I'm grateful for …
6. My strongest sense, image, moment, or experience of God's loving presence so far has been …

Now go back to your journal entries from the First Sunday of Advent and the first couple of days of the journey.

1. What did I desire as I began this journey? Have those desires grown or changed in some way?
2. How has God answered the prayers that I prayed at the beginning of Advent?
3. Do I notice a particular theme that has been emerging on my *Oriens* pilgrimage?
4. Do I have recurring fears or struggles that Jesus is wanting to address with me?
5. Today is also New Year's Eve. How did God bless me in 2022? Perhaps flip back through the pictures on your phone and recall where you and God have been together.
6. As I look back on 2022, and then forward to next year, what is the one lesson or insight from this year that will change the way I live 2023? What concrete steps do I need to take to implement this change?

Conclude by conversing with God about your week. **Acknowledge** what you have been experiencing. **Relate** it to him. **Receive** what he wants to give you. **Respond** to him. Then savor that image of God's loving presence and rest there for a minute or two. Close with an Our Father.

Week Six

Well Begun Is Half Done

On my thirty-day silent retreat, I was introduced to the words of Saint Ignatius. He told retreatants to begin each prayer time by "pausing for the space of an Our Father and considering how God our Lord looks upon us." I wasn't sure how to do that. I tried various images of God's love, but it never really clicked for me, nor for the people I directed on retreats. I didn't want to let it go, though. If we don't start prayer by realizing we are not alone, we might never actually get to conversation with God. Prayer will become nothing more than a conversation with myself, as I read spiritual things and think up spiritual thoughts and goals for myself.

While writing this book, I toyed with a variety of different ways to start the prayer time. I eventually realized that once you have had an experience of God's loving care for you, you can keep "recycling" that experience by starting your next day from that place. Saint Ignatius wasn't inviting us to invent how God might look at us, but rather to return to a place, prayer image, or Scripture passage where we have encountered God's love.

God never stops loving us. The sun will stop shining before God stops loving you. But we don't always feel his love. Today I might feel burdened, distracted, lost, confused, or even abandoned. However, God and I have a history together; I have experienced his loving care in the past, and I am sure to experience it again in the future. So, I begin my prayer by remembering a time that I felt particularly loved, blessed, and cared for. This helps me enter back into that moment and begin my prayer from a place of gratitude.

Before we finish our prayer time, we should end with gratitude. When we realize what God has done for us, how he has loved us faithfully and sent his Son to die for us, we cannot help but feel grateful. Gratitude is the antidote to anger, the antithesis of a consumer mentality, and the right attitude of a disciple. Our prayer should begin and end with gratitude.

Mother Church has the same idea when we traditionally pray both a grace before meals and a grace after meals. Our meals, however meager they may be, begin and end with gratitude. The Church's Morning Prayer is called "Morning Praises" (*laudes*) to begin our day with gratitude. Night Prayer ends with a hymn to Our Lady, an act of gratitude for her maternal care. The word Eucharist means "thanksgiving," as we begin and end our week with gratitude. For the last several years, I have kept a quart jar in my prayer space. Every Saturday, I write down the thing I am most grateful for and put it in the jar. At the end of the year, I dump out the jar and sift through all my blessings. Our meals, prayer time, days, weeks, and years should begin and end with gratitude.

Grace of the Week: We will journey through the last official week of Christmas to the feasts of Epiphany and the Baptism of the Lord. Our guide will be the beloved disciple, who wrote the Gospel of John and three letters. He has a deep sense of God's love for us and a desire that we remain in that love and not reject it. Ask God for the grace to help you experience and live more deeply your true identity as a beloved child of God.

January 1 — Sunday
The Blessed Virgin Mary, the Mother of God

EIGHTH DAY IN THE OCTAVE OF CHRISTMAS

Preparation: *Come, Holy Spirit, enlighten the eyes of my heart.* Be present to the God who is always present to you. Call to mind his loving care for you and spend the first minute of your prayer just resting in the free, unearned gift of loving and being loved. Let gratitude rise in your heart.

Lectio: Ask God for the grace to help you experience and live more deeply your true identity as a beloved child of God. The title of Mary as "Mother of God" officially entered the Church's vocabulary in AD 431 at the Council of Ephesus. Jesus is one person with two distinct natures, a human nature and a divine nature. Since Mary was Jesus' mother, and Jesus is God, is it proper to call Mary the Mother of God? Nestorius, patriarch of Constantinople, argued that God has no mother, and so Mary should only be referred to as the Mother of Christ. Cyril, the patriarch of Alexandria, disagreed. The pope supported Cyril, and the emperor supported Nestorius. Approximately 250 bishops gathered in Ephesus for what became known as the Third Ecumenical Council. The bishops sided with Cyril against Nestorius. Jesus does have two distinct natures, but a mother gives birth to a person, not a nature. Mary is the mother of a person who is God, and therefore Mary is the Mother of God. You may never have thought about what these words really mean, let alone that they could ignite such controversy. Be prepared to think more deeply as you read today's Scripture passage slowly and prayerfully.

GALATIANS 4:4–7 (LECTIONARY)

Brothers and sisters:
When the fullness of time had come, God sent his Son,
born of a woman, born under the law,
to ransom those under the law,
so that we might receive adoption as sons.

> *As proof that you are sons,*
> *God sent the Spirit of his Son into our hearts,*
> *crying out, "Abba, Father!"*
> *So you are no longer a slave but a son,*
> *and if a son then also an heir, through God.*

Meditatio: By nature human, you are destined for divinity. By a kind of marvelous exchange, God has taken on humanity so that we can receive his divinity. In his 1881 book, *The Prince and the Pauper*, Mark Twain imagines a poor orphan switching places with the heir to the throne of England. This is exactly how Saint Paul understands the Incarnation. Jesus has entered the world disguised as a beggar and offered to switch places with us. He dies the death of a wretched sinner, and we are welcomed into the kingdom of God. What thoughts and feelings arise inside of you as you imagine such unimaginable generosity, such incredibly divine mercy? Read the passage a second time.

Oratio: The very Mother of God, Mary herself, is but a poor and lowly handmaid whom God raised to the dignity of the Queen of Heaven. Now she intercedes for all God's children and helps them be worthy of their high calling. In a sense, Mary trains us for heaven. Ask Mary to help you truly accept your dignity as a child of God. Picture God himself as a kind, loving, and thoughtful Father. Speak to him from your heart. The Spirit will help you. If you get stuck with this image and find it hard to relate to God in this way, ask Mary to help you.

Contemplatio: What does it mean to God that you are his child and he is your Father? Read the passage a third time very slowly and allow these words to enter your heart. Rest in your Father's love for you for a few minutes before moving on.

SUGGESTIONS FOR JOURNALING
1. I find it hard to accept the idea that …
2. My heart leapt for joy when …
3. My biggest obstacle to accepting the Fatherhood of God is …

4. My heart rested when …
5. In this new year, my deepest desire is …

_____

_____

_____

_____

_____

_____

_____

_____

_____

_____

_____

_____

_____

_____

After you've journaled, close with a brief conversation with your Father and your Mother, giving thanks for your prayer experience. Then pray an Our Father from your heart, truly meaning each word of the prayer that Jesus himself taught God's children.

Monday Before Epiphany

SAINTS BASIL THE GREAT AND
GREGORY NAZIANZEN, BISHOPS AND
DOCTORS OF THE CHURCH

Basil was a brilliant student from a Christian family in Cappadocia (present-day Turkey). He was on his way to a great career as a teacher when he resigned and went to found what was probably the first monastery in Asia Minor. He became an archbishop and a famous orator who preached to large crowds. When Saint Athanasius died, Basil inherited the defense of orthodoxy against the Arian heresy. He died at the age of forty-nine.

Gregory was also from Cappadocia. He and Basil became friends at school. He followed Basil into monastic life. A retiring and sensitive soul, he was drawn into the Arian conflict when Basil ordained him bishop and sent him to rescue a diocese that was slipping into Arianism. After Basil's death, Gregory became the first orthodox bishop of Constantinople in thirty years. His brilliant sermons on the Trinity won him the nickname "the Theologian." He hated all the conflict and finally retired to a quiet life of prayer, meditation, and writing. Both are honored as Doctors (teachers) of the Church.

Preparation: *Come, Holy Spirit, enlighten the eyes of my heart.* Be present to the God who is always present to you. Call to mind his loving care for you and spend the first minute of your prayer just resting in the free, unearned gift of loving and being loved. Let gratitude rise in your heart.

Lectio: Ask God for the grace to help you experience and live more deeply your true identity as a beloved child of God. Falling in love happens suddenly and often without warning. We suddenly realize we have been swept off our feet by beauty, truth, and goodness. Falling out of love happens slowly and not without warning. Little frustrations build up due to poor communication and lack of quality time together. Habits of isolation develop. We realize that the person we once loved has become a stranger to us. Love must be protected, nurtured, and cherished. Saint John is concerned that we who are beloved by God might fall out of love with God. See the love that John has for the people to whom he is writing this letter and his deep desire for them to have the very best. Read the passage slowly and prayerfully.

1 JOHN 2:22–28

Who is the liar? Whoever denies that Jesus is the Christ. Whoever denies the Father and the Son, this is the antichrist. Anyone who denies the Son does not have the Father, but whoever confesses the Son has the Father as well.

Let what you heard from the beginning remain in you. If what you heard from the beginning remains in you, then you will remain in the Son and in the Father. And this is the promise that he made us: eternal life. I write you these things about those who would deceive you. As for you, the anointing that you received from him remains in you, so that you do not need anyone to teach you. But his anointing teaches you about everything and is true and not false; just as it taught you, remain in him.

And now, children, remain in him, so that when he appears we may have confidence and not be put to shame by him at his coming.

Meditatio: "The anointing you received from him" refers to the Holy Spirit given at our baptism and again in the Sacrament of Confirmation. You cannot lose the sacrament, but you can lose touch with the Holy Spirit. Has the time, effort, and energy you once put into prayer begun to wane? Are you finding yourself slipping into old habits again? What would you have to do, or not do, to remain in the Son and in the Father, and have confidence and not be put to shame at his coming? Read the passage again.

Oratio: The Holy Spirit is with you. He will help you to know what it is that you most deeply desire. "Draw near to God and he will draw near to you" (Jas 4:8). Speak to the Father, or to the Son, in the Holy Spirit. Reclaim your identity as a beloved, welcomed, and cherished member of the Holy Trinity by your adoption into the Son. Be honest and open; be not afraid.

Contemplatio: Read the passage again. This time receive from God's Holy Spirit. Spend a little while abiding in God and letting God abide in you. Remain in him for a few minutes right here and right now.

SUGGESTIONS FOR JOURNALING

1. How have I experienced the love of the Father and the Son for me?
2. Have I remained in that love? What has caused me to wander from that love?
3. Where do I hear the voices of the world, the flesh, or the Devil seeking to deceive me by denying that I am beloved?
4. I felt the Spirit of God present within me when …
5. What helps me to remain in God's love is …

_____

_____

_____

_____

_____

_____

_____

_____

_____

_____

_____

_____

_____

_____

_____

_____

_____

_____

_____

_____

After you've journaled, close with a brief moment of gratitude and thanksgiving for today's prayer experience. Join with the Son and pray an Our Father in the Spirit of your adopted sonship.

January 3 — Tuesday
Tuesday Before Epiphany

THE HOLY NAME OF JESUS

Mary and Joseph were both instructed by angels to name their child "Jesus" (Lk 1:31, Mt 1:21). It was pronounced Y'shua in his native Aramaic and ΙΗΣΟΥΣ (YE-SOUS) in the Greek language of the New Testament. This is "the name that is above every name, that at the name of Jesus every knee should bend, of those in heaven and on earth and under the earth" (Phil 2:9b–10). St. Bernardine of Siena preached on the Holy Name of Jesus using the monogram IHS (transliterated from the first three letters of Jesus' name in Greek) and added the name of Jesus to the Hail Mary. This feast was added to the universal calendar in 1721, dropped in the reform after Vatican II, and re-added by Pope St. John Paul II.

Preparation: *Come, Holy Spirit, enlighten the eyes of my heart.* Be present to the God who is always present to you. Call to mind his loving care for you and spend the first minute of your prayer just resting in the free, unearned gift of loving and being loved. Let gratitude rise in your heart.

Lectio: Ask God for the grace to help you experience and live more deeply your true identity as a beloved child of God. Today's passage is full of deep, rich ideas. Read it slowly and savor it. Notice what speaks to your heart.

1 JOHN 2:29—3:6 (LECTIONARY)

If you consider that God is righteous,
you also know that everyone who acts in righteousness
is begotten by him.

See what love the Father has bestowed on us
that we may be called the children of God.
Yet so we are.
The reason the world does not know us is that it did not

> *know him.*
> *Beloved, we are God's children now;*
> *what we shall be has not yet been revealed.*
> *We do know that when it is revealed we shall be like him,*
> *for we shall see him as he is.*
> *Everyone who has this hope based on him makes himself*
>   *pure,*
> *as he is pure.*
>
> *Everyone who commits sin commits lawlessness,*
> *for sin is lawlessness.*
> *You know that he was revealed to take away sins,*
> *and in him there is no sin.*
> *No one who remains in him sins;*
> *no one who sins has seen him or known him.*

Meditatio: Imagine for a moment being a poor orphan who was adopted by a rich and powerful man. This man had only one natural son, but he wanted to share his riches with other children. Having been adopted into the rich family, you would be expected to live in a manner worthy of your new family. The natural son would be your example for how to act. In a similar way, we have been adopted into God's family. God is good, and we are called to be good like God. When have you failed to live up to this noble calling? How can you draw strength to love from the one who is Love itself? Chew on these ideas, then read the passage again.

Oratio: We might think that God is trying to make us into something we are not. In reality, though, God is trying to help us be what we were created to be. You were created "in the beginning" to be God's beloved children. Through the envy of the Devil, we fell from grace and became convinced that we were not worthy of the Name of Jesus. But that is not true. God sent his Son to restore us to our original dignity. He then gave us the same Spirit that descended on Jesus and remains in him. It is the Spirit dwelling in you that enables you to live a righteous, pure, and holy life — the life you were created for! What desires arise in your heart? What fears or doubts? Bring them all to God; you can be completely honest with him. He already knows it all, he's just waiting for you to admit it.

Contemplatio: Read the passage a third time. How does God respond to your thoughts, feelings, and desires? How does he reassure you? Can you receive what God wants to give you? Receive God's love and abide in that love for a few minutes before moving on. Savor the love of the one in whose name you have been saved and sealed for eternal life.

SUGGESTIONS FOR JOURNALING

1. What does it mean to me to be called a child of God? What does it mean to be "like him, for we shall see him as he is"?
2. My strongest thought, feeling, or desire was …
3. I have a hard time believing that …
4. I need the Spirit to help me …
5. I ended prayer with a deep sense of …

After you've journaled, close with a brief conversation thanking God for your adoption and for your time in prayer today. Then say the Name of Jesus nine times, slowly and prayerfully, as a closing prayer.

January 4 — Wednesday
Wednesday before Epiphany

SAINT ELIZABETH ANN SETON, RELIGIOUS (USA)

Born in New York in 1774, Elizabeth grew up in the Anglican church. At an early age, she learned the value of prayer, Scripture, and the nightly examination of conscience. The belle of New York high society, she married a handsome, wealthy businessman with whom she had five children. His business failed, and he died of tuberculosis, leaving her a penniless widow by the age of thirty. The kindness of Catholic friends during her husband's death opened her heart to the Catholic Church. She was drawn by the Eucharist, devotion to Mother Mary, and a conviction that the Catholic Church led back to the apostles and to Jesus. Many friends rejected her when she became Catholic in March 1805. She opened a school, the first American Catholic orphanage, and eventually a religious order. "Mother Seton," as she became known, died on this day in 1821. Her journey had taken her from ordinary goodness to heroic sanctity, and to becoming the first American-born citizen to be beatified and canonized a saint.

Preparation: *Come, Holy Spirit, enlighten the eyes of my heart.* Be present to the God who is always present to you. Call to mind his loving care for you and spend the first minute of your prayer just resting in the free, unearned gift of loving and being loved. Let gratitude rise in your heart.

Set the Scene: Ask for the grace of a deepening sense of your identity as a beloved child of God, and to hear Jesus inviting you to come and see. The Synoptic Gospels (Matthew, Mark, and Luke) depict the call of the first disciples as a sudden, immediate moment. Jesus says, "Come, follow me," and they leave everything and follow him. John's Gospel shows a more gradual introduction. Andrew and John had already been following John the Baptist as he prepared the way for the Messiah. They move from following the forerunner to following the Lamb of God himself. The popular Bible series called *The Chosen* depicts Jesus camping in the woods. Where do you picture that Jesus is staying? Use your imagination to set the scene: John the Baptist, clothed in camel's hair, his disciples leaving him to follow Jesus, then hanging out with Jesus that afternoon. Read the passage slowly and prayerfully.

JOHN 1:35–42 (LECTIONARY)

John was standing with two of his disciples,
and as he watched Jesus walk by, he said,
"Behold, the Lamb of God."
The two disciples heard what he said and followed Jesus.
Jesus turned and saw them following him and said to them, "What are you looking for?"
They said to him, "Rabbi" (which translated means Teacher), "where are you staying?"
He said to them, "Come, and you will see."
So they went and saw where he was staying,
and they stayed with him that day.
It was about four in the afternoon.
Andrew, the brother of Simon Peter,
was one of the two who heard John and followed Jesus.
He first found his own brother Simon and told him,
"We have found the Messiah," which is translated Christ.
Then he brought him to Jesus.
Jesus looked at him and said,
"You are Simon the son of John;
you will be called Cephas," which is translated Peter.

Action! The nation of Israel is eagerly awaiting the promised Messiah (Hebrew for "Anointed One"). John has gone ahead to prepare the way *in the spirit and power of Elijah.* He is the voice crying out in the wilderness, the finger that points to "one mightier than I." This moment must have had an impact on these two disciples, as John remembers the exact time it happened, and Andrew ran to get his brother and tell him the good news. What was it like to hang out with Jesus that afternoon? Use your imagination and hang out with them. Read the passage again.

Acknowledge: What does it feel like to remain with Jesus that afternoon? What thoughts go through your mind? What desires are stirred up in your soul?

Relate: If you could hang out with Jesus the whole afternoon, what would you say? Speak to Jesus honestly; don't worry about what the others will think.

Receive: How does Jesus receive what you have to say? How does he respond to you? Can you sense his love for you? Read the passage a third time.

Respond: What is Jesus inviting you to, drawing you to, or offering you? What does he want from you? Is it easy to be with him, or does it make you uncomfortable? Say yes to whatever Jesus is doing, then savor his friendship for a few minutes.

SUGGESTIONS FOR JOURNALING

1. What thoughts, feelings, desires, worries, and fears emerged in my heart when John said, "Behold the Lamb of God?"
2. How did I feel when Jesus turned and looked at me?
3. What did I think and feel as we spent the afternoon together?
4. Jesus wanted me to know that …
5. I ended prayer wanting …

After you've journaled, close with a brief conversation thanking Jesus for the time together today, then join John, Andrew, Peter, and the Master in praying one Our Father all together.

Thursday Before Epiphany

SAINT JOHN NEUMANN, BISHOP (USA)

Born in 1811 in Bohemia (the western half of the present-day Czech Republic), John felt a desire to be an American missionary. He was ordained in New York in 1834. He worked to establish parishes and schools in Maryland, Virginia, and Ohio. He became bishop of Philadelphia at the age of forty-one and organized the parochial school system that helped define the Catholic experience in the United States.

Preparation: *Come, Holy Spirit, enlighten the eyes of my heart.* Be present to the God who is always present to you. Call to mind his loving care for you and spend the first minute of your prayer just resting in the free, unearned gift of loving and being loved. Let gratitude rise in your heart.

Set the Scene: Ask for the grace of a deepening sense of your identity as a beloved child of God, and to hear Jesus inviting you to follow him. The next morning (after yesterday's Gospel with the calling of Peter, Andrew, and John), Jesus continues to call two more disciples. Bethsaida is thought to be a town near where the Jordan River flows southward out of the Sea of Galilee. No sooner has Philip been called then he goes and finds Nathanael and invites him, too, to follow Jesus. Picture the fig tree and each character in the story as you read the passage below.

JOHN 1:43–51 (LECTIONARY)

Jesus decided to go to Galilee, and he found Philip.
And Jesus said to him, "Follow me."
Now Philip was from Bethsaida, the town of Andrew and Peter.
Philip found Nathanael and told him,
"We have found the one about whom Moses wrote in the law, and also the prophets, Jesus, son of Joseph, from Nazareth." But Nathanael said to him,

"Can anything good come from Nazareth?"
Philip said to him, "Come and see."
Jesus saw Nathanael coming toward him and said of him,
"Here is a true child of Israel.
There is no duplicity in him."
Nathanael said to him, "How do you know me?"
Jesus answered and said to him,
"Before Philip called you, I saw you under the fig tree."
Nathanael answered him,
"Rabbi, you are the Son of God; you are the King of Israel."
Jesus answered and said to him,
"Do you believe because I told you that I saw you under
   the fig tree?
You will see greater things than this."
And he said to him, "Amen, amen, I say to you,
you will see the sky opened and the angels of God
ascending and descending on the Son of Man."

Action! This passage is full of allusions to the history of the Jewish people. Abraham's grandson Jacob was a trickster who tricked his brother
Esau out of his father's blessing (see Gn 27). On his journey to find himself a wife from his own kinfolk, he has a dream in which he sees the
angels of God ascending and descending, the famous "Jacob's ladder"
(Gn 28:10–22). Toward the end of his life, God gives Jacob the new name
"Israel" (Gn 32:29). Jesus is here presented as the new "Jacob's ladder,"
the connecting point between heaven and earth. Read the passage again.
This time notice what each character is thinking or feeling.

Acknowledge: Does this passage encourage, confuse, or intrigue you?
Do you feel seen and known by God, as Nathanael was? Does that feeling comfort you or make you uncomfortable? What thought, feeling, or
desire do you notice most strongly? Just notice what is going on inside
of you.

Relate: Turn to Jesus. Speak to him honestly, from your heart, with "no
duplicity."

Receive: What is in Jesus' heart for you? Read the passage a third time. This time focus on Jesus and notice whatever it is he wants to say to you or give you.

Respond: Continue the conversation with Jesus. If you received something from Jesus, respond to it. If you received nothing from Jesus, tell him how that makes you feel. After an honest conversation, enjoy his presence for a few minutes before moving on.

SUGGESTIONS FOR JOURNALING

1. When have I felt seen and known by God?
2. When have I heard the voice of Jesus calling me to "follow him" in the ordinary experiences of my life, through my prayer time, or through the sacraments?
3. What did it feel like to be called by Jesus? How did I respond? If I haven't felt the call of Jesus, what does that feel like? What do I desire to hear?
4. Do I feel comfortable with Jesus?
5. Does Jesus feel comfortable with me?

_____

_____

_____

_____

_____

_____

_____

_____

_____

_____

_____

_____

_____

_____

_____

_____

After you've journaled, close with a brief conversation thanking Jesus for his friendship and for your prayer experience today. Then pray an Our Father.

January 6 — Friday

The Epiphany of the Lord (Traditional)

The name Epiphany means "manifestation." Through the arrival of the wise men (magi) from the East, Jesus is manifest as not only the King of the Jews, but as the Savior of all peoples and a light for all the nations. The Eastern churches refer to this day as "Little Christmas" or "Theophany." Many cultures have special traditions associated with this feast, including parades, special foods, and gift-giving. In the United States, the liturgical celebration of the Epiphany is always transferred to the Sunday between January 2 and January 8. However, there's no reason we cannot celebrate this feast also on its proper day.

Preparation: *Come, Holy Spirit, enlighten the eyes of my heart.* Be present to the God who is always present to you. Call to mind his loving care for you and spend the first minute of your prayer just resting in the free, unearned gift of loving and being loved. Let gratitude rise in your heart.

Lectio: Pray for the grace of a deepening sense of your identity as a beloved child of God, and to serve the true king and experience the peace of his kingdom. The notes for the *New American Bible* explain today's passages, saying, "A royal Psalm in which the Israelite king, as the representative of God, is the instrument of divine justice and blessing for the whole world." The extravagant, superlative language would be typical of royal courts in the ancient Near East. Is it too much to hope for a king who rules with justice and peace and cares for the poor? Not if this king is the Son of God! Picture Jesus seated on the lap of his mother as the magi do him homage and present him with gifts. Read the passage slowly and prayerfully.

PSALM 72:1–2, 7–8, 10–11, 12–13 (LECTIONARY)

O God, with your judgment endow the king,
and with your justice, the king's son;

He shall govern your people with justice
and your afflicted ones with judgment.
Justice shall flower in his days,
and profound peace, till the moon be no more.
May he rule from sea to sea,
and from the River to the ends of the earth.
The kings of Tarshish and the Isles shall offer gifts;
the kings of Arabia and Seba shall bring tribute.
All kings shall pay him homage,
all nations shall serve him.
For he shall rescue the poor when he cries out,
and the afflicted when he has no one to help him.
He shall have pity for the lowly and the poor;
the lives of the poor he shall save.

Meditatio: Tarshish and the islands sit to the far west of Israel; Sheba and Seba to the distant southeast. Even these distant kingdoms have not only heard of the king, but also come to pay tribute to him. In what ways does the kingdom of Jesus Christ extend "to the ends of the earth"? How does he rescue the poor when they cry out? Meditate on how this psalm has come true in ways the psalmist could not have imagined. Then read the passage a second time.

Oratio: What do you have to offer God? What gifts can you lay before the king? Search the treasury of your heart for the thing Jesus most wants to receive from you. Picture yourself entering the house as the fourth wise man, or perhaps as one of the poor that Jesus desires to save. Speak to him from your heart.

Contemplatio: Read the passage a third time. What does Jesus want to give you: peace, justice, rescue, pity? He is a generous king and has gifts in abundance for you. Receive whatever is in the king's heart for you. Rejoice and praise him for his goodness. Perhaps it is your friendship that he most desires. Rejoice in his humble presence with you for a few minutes before moving on.

SUGGESTIONS FOR JOURNALING

1. The phrase from the psalm that most spoke to me was …
2. When I see Jesus as a king, I think of …
3. I wanted to give Jesus …
4. Jesus wanted to give me …
5. I ended prayer with a stronger or deeper sense of …

After you've journaled, close with a brief conversation thanking the King for your prayer time today. Then pray an Our Father.

+

Bless your home today, or plan ahead for a blessing party on Sunday. Instructions follow on the next page.

Blessing of the Home and Household on Epiphany

The custom of blessing homes while recalling the visit of the magi is celebrated in many Old World countries. The C, M, and B of the inscription refer to the traditional names of the three wise men: Caspar, Melchior, and Balthasar. The numbers are the date of the current year. The family gathers. Candles are lit. It is most appropriate to gather around the Advent wreath in which the purple candles have been replaced with white, but any white, non-scented candles may be lit.

The leader (preferably the father or eldest resident) begins by saying:

> Peace be with this house and with all who live here. Blessed be the name of the Lord!
>
> During these days of the Christmas season, we keep this feast of Epiphany, celebrating the manifestation of Christ to the Magi. Today, Christ is manifest to us! Today, this home is a holy place.

Let us pray:

> Father, we give you special thanks on this festival of the Epiphany, for leading the Magi from afar to the home of Christ, who has given light and hope to all peoples.
>
> By the power of the Holy Spirit, may his presence be renewed in our home.
>
> Make our home a place of human wholeness and divine holiness: a place of joy and laughter, a place of forgiveness and peace, a place of prayer, service, and discipleship.

The leader takes the blessed chalk and marks the lintel (the doorframe above the door) on the inside of the main entrance to the house as follows:

20 + C + M + B + 23
(insert the last two digits of the current year)

The prayer below is said during the marking by another family member, such as the other parent or a child:

> Loving God, as we mark this lintel, send the angel of mercy to guard our home and repel all powers of darkness. Fill those of us living here with a love for each other and warm us with the fullness of your presence and love.

After the lintel has been marked, the leader finishes by saying:

> Lord our God, you revealed your only-begotten Son to every nation by the guidance of a star.
> Bless now this household with health, goodness of heart, gentleness, and the keeping of your law of love.
> May all who visit this dwelling find here:
> the tender loving care of Mary, the God-bearer, the prayerful protection of Saint Joseph, the faithful perseverance of the magi, and the humble peace of the Christ Child,
> the light of the nations, and thus praise you for all eternity in the unity of the Holy Spirit and the Church, now and forever.

All respond: Amen.

All join hands and pray together the Our Father. The leader then invites all to share a sign of peace.

Other doors may be marked by family members, especially children marking the doors of their own bedrooms. If possible, the family may continue the celebration by sharing a special meal together.

January 7 — Saturday
Saturday Before Epiphany

SAINT ANDRÉ BESSETTE (CANADA)

Born August 9, 1845, to a French Canadian couple, he was the eighth of twelve children. By the time he was twelve, both his parents had died, leaving him an orphan. He developed a deep devotion to Saint Joseph. At the age of twenty-five, he applied to the Congregation of the Holy Cross. Weak health extended his novitiate, but he was finally accepted and given the job of doorkeeper at Notre Dame College in Montreal. He would joke, "When I joined this community, the superiors showed me the door, and I remained forty years." The sick came to be prayed for and many were healed. When an epidemic broke out in a nearby hospital, he volunteered to nurse the sick, and not a single person died. His healing powers became famous, though he always gave credit to Saint Joseph. He died on January 6, 1937, and was buried in the magnificent oratory on Mont Royal that was the fruit of his labors and faith. He is celebrated on January 6 in the United States and on January 7 in his home country.

REVIEW

Preparation: *Come, Holy Spirit, enlighten the eyes of my heart.* Call to mind God's loving care for you this past week and spend the first minute of your prayer just resting in the free, unearned gift of loving and being loved. Let gratitude rise in your heart.

We made a journey through John's first letter and his account of being called by Jesus. Did you feel called by Jesus? Flip back through your past week's journal entries. As you do, notice what emerged in the conversation. Here are some questions to help you:

1. Where did I notice God, and what was he doing or saying?
2. How did I respond to what God was doing?
3. I felt most like a child of God when …
4. I struggle to see myself as a child of God when (or because) …
5. I'm grateful for …

6. I feel called to …
7. This past week, my strongest sense, image, moment, or experience of God's loving presence was …

_____

_____

_____

_____

_____

_____

_____

_____

_____

_____

_____

_____

_____

_____

_____

_____

_____

_____

Conclude by conversing with God about your week. **Acknowledge** what you have been experiencing. **Relate** it to him. **Receive** what he wants to give you. **Respond** to him. Then savor that image of God's loving presence and rest there for a minute or two. Close with an Our Father.

Week Seven

Keep the Christmas Light Burning Brightly

The traditional American celebration of Christmas begins as early as possible and ends on Christmas Day. In contrast, the Catholic celebration starts on Christmas Day. Officially, the Catholic celebration ends on the feast of the Baptism of the Lord (usually a Sunday, except when Epiphany is transferred forward to January 7 or 8). It seems that our ancestors were fond of making Christmas last for forty days. In medieval and Tudor England, homes would be decorated with greenery such as laurel, holly, ivy, and rosemary at Christmas time. It was left decorating the house until Candlemas Eve. Candlemas is the old English name for the feast of the Presentation, celebrated on February 2. This was the day that Jesus was presented in the Temple (see Lk 2:22–40). My first year as I priest, I turned to February 2 in the Roman Missal and was taken aback. The instructions said to begin outside of church with the blessing of candles and process into church carrying lit candles. Clearly, this feast used to be a big deal. But why?

Lit candles are a symbol of faith. Baby Jesus has lit our hearts on fire, and now we are shining with heavenly light. The procession reminds us of the wise virgins (see Mt 25:1–13) and all the biblical admonitions to be ready and waiting for the Master's return. They harken back to the candles on the Advent wreath that lit up our home as the world grew darker. They also foreshadow the candlelight procession of the Easter Vigil. Just as we have forty days of Lent followed by fifty days of Easter, celebrating Candlemas gives us up to twenty-eight days of Advent followed by forty days of Christmas. I think the celebration of Christmas makes more sense when it ends on Candlemas. We need the lights and cheer especially during the dreary days of January. And the waiting of Advent makes more sense when you can savor a longer Christmas.

Even though the liturgical season of Christmas will be over, your own personal celebration can continue. I encourage you to keep your Advent wreath and Nativity scene up in the spirit of the old English tradition. Keep praying and keep savoring the light of Christ shining from the manger scene. God has more to give. Let us keep our hearts open to receive.

Grace of the Week: This week we will return to Ordinary Time, both in the liturgical season and in our lives. Our readings are drawn from the daily Mass readings. We have seen God present in the shining moments of Christmas. His ordinary presence may be less bright, but keep your eyes open and you will find him no less present. Ask God for the grace to welcome Jesus into your home and to follow him more faithfully in the new year.

January 8 — Sunday
The Epiphany of the Lord (Observed)

Preparation: *Come, Holy Spirit, enlighten the eyes of my heart.* Be present to the God who is always present to you. Call to mind his loving care for you and spend the first minute of your prayer just resting in the free, unearned gift of loving and being loved. Let gratitude rise in your heart.

Set the Scene: Ask God for the grace to welcome Jesus into your home and to follow him more faithfully into the new year. Read through this passage slowly and prayerfully. Spend some time really setting the scene. What is the city like? What do the magi look like? Picture the camels threading their way through the streets of Jerusalem, then Bethlehem. What does the house look like where the mother and child are?

MATTHEW 2:1–12 (LECTIONARY)

When Jesus was born in Bethlehem of Judea,
in the days of King Herod,
behold, magi from the east arrived in Jerusalem, saying,
"Where is the newborn king of the Jews?
We saw his star at its rising
and have come to do him homage."
When King Herod heard this,
he was greatly troubled,
and all Jerusalem with him.
Assembling all the chief priests and the scribes of the people, he inquired of them where the Christ was to be born.
They said to him, "In Bethlehem of Judea,
for thus it has been written through the prophet:
'And you, Bethlehem, land of Judah,
are by no means least among the rulers of Judah;
since from you shall come a ruler,
who is to shepherd my people Israel.'"

Then Herod called the magi secretly
and ascertained from them the time of the star's appear-
ance. He sent them to Bethlehem and said,
"Go and search diligently for the child.
When you have found him, bring me word,
that I too may go and do him homage."
After their audience with the king they set out.
And behold, the star that they had seen at its rising
*   preceded them,*
until it came and stopped over the place where the child
was. They were overjoyed at seeing the star,
and on entering the house
they saw the child with Mary his mother.
They prostrated themselves and did him homage.
Then they opened their treasures
and offered him gifts of gold, frankincense, and myrrh.
And having been warned in a dream not to return to
Herod, they departed for their country by another way.

Action! The magi have made quite the pilgrimage. What was it like? Did they experience frustration? How did they encourage each other? What goes through their minds and hearts as they finally arrive? They find the child with his mother. Picture the relationship between mother and child. Read the passage a second time and let the scene unfold in your imagination.

Acknowledge: You, too, have been on a pilgrimage. What thoughts, feelings, and desires are rising in your heart?

Relate: Share your thoughts and feelings with Mary, the Mother of God. How does she respond to you?

Receive: Read the passage a third time. What does the mother want to tell you about her Son? What does she want to tell you about yourself? What is in Mary's heart for you?

Respond: You have a gift to give. Open your treasures and respond by giving the Christ Child your gift.

SUGGESTIONS FOR JOURNALING

1. This time I was most drawn to ...
2. I was particularly moved by ...
3. The gift I want to give Jesus is ...
4. I have been encouraged on this journey by ...
5. Who have I encouraged on their pilgrimage of faith?

_____

_____

_____

_____

_____

_____

_____

_____

_____

_____

_____

_____

_____

_____

_____

After you've journaled, close by spending a minute thanking God for your prayer experience today. Then pray a Hail Mary.

+

If you haven't blessed your home already, instructions may be found back on pages 207–208.

January 9 — Monday
Baptism of the Lord

The Baptism of the Lord is ordinarily celebrated on the Sunday after Epiphany. But when Epiphany is moved to January 7 or 8, the baptism is then celebrated on the Monday immediately following Epiphany. Jesus' baptism reveals the Holy Trinity and also marks the end of his so-called "hidden life" and the beginning of his public ministry. This feast ends the liturgical celebration of Christmas and begins the season of Ordinary Time.

Preparation: *Come, Holy Spirit, enlighten the eyes of my heart.* Be present to the God who is always present to you. Call to mind his loving care for you and spend the first minute of your prayer just resting in the free, unearned gift of loving and being loved. Let gratitude rise in your heart.

Set the Scene: Ask God for the grace to welcome Jesus into your home and to follow him more faithfully in the new year. John the Baptist has been preaching in the wilderness of Judea, telling the people: "Repent, for the kingdom of heaven is at hand" (Mt 3:2). He wears a rough garment of camel's hair and feeds on locusts and wild honey. Picture the people coming out into the wilderness from the city of Jerusalem and the region of Judea, listening to John preaching, confessing their sins, and being baptized in the Jordan River. Among the throng of sinners stands the one mightier than John, whose sandals he is not worthy to carry (see Mt 3:11). Read the passage and use your imagination to set the scene.

MATTHEW 3:13-17 (LECTIONARY)
Jesus came from Galilee to John at the Jordan
to be baptized by him.
John tried to prevent him, saying,
"I need to be baptized by you,
and yet you are coming to me?"
Jesus said to him in reply,
"Allow it now, for thus it is fitting for us

to fulfill all righteousness."
Then he allowed him.
After Jesus was baptized,
he came up from the water and behold,
the heavens were opened for him,
and he saw the Spirit of God descending like a dove
and coming upon him.
And a voice came from the heavens, saying,
"This is my beloved Son, with whom I am well pleased."

Action! The baptism that John offers is a visible sign of new life. People confess their sins and resolve to do better. They drown their old life in the waters of the river and come out the other side a new person, or at least a person committed to a better way of life. Pharisees and Sadducees are coming for baptism, but with no desire to start a new life because they think they are already righteous (see Mt 3:7–10). Among all the sinners stands Jesus himself, the sinless one. Surely, Jesus is the one man who doesn't need to be baptized. John pauses as he seems to notice this incongruity. Why does Jesus choose to join the sinners? Why does he receive baptism? Ponder these questions as you read the passage a second time and play through the scene in your imagination.

Acknowledge: Put yourself in the scene. Where are you? Do you, too, line up for baptism, or are you afraid to confess your sins, or do you see yourself as already righteous? Notice the thoughts and feelings inside of you. Welcome them without judging them.

Relate: Jesus is with you, perhaps drying off in the hot sun. Sit with Jesus by the Jordan River. Share with him what is on your heart.

Receive: How does Jesus respond? Listen to Jesus' heart. What did Jesus' baptism mean for him? Many of us were baptized when we were too young to remember it. What does Jesus want to teach you about your baptism? Be open to whatever God is offering — a word, thought, or feeling, a new understanding or insight. Read the passage a third time and see this moment, and yourself, through Jesus' eyes.

Respond: Continue the conversation for a little while. Then just rest in the love God has for you, the same love that the Father has for his only begotten Son.

SUGGESTIONS FOR JOURNALING

1. The part that stood out to me from today's reading was …
2. My most prominent thought, feeling, or desire was …
3. Jesus wanted to show me or teach me …
4. I ended prayer wanting …
5. I now see my own baptism in a new way …

After you've journaled, close with a brief conversation giving thanks to God, Father, Son, and Spirit for your prayer experience. Then pray an Our Father.

January 10 — Tuesday
Tuesday of the First Week in Ordinary Time

Preparation: *Come, Holy Spirit, enlighten the eyes of my heart.* Be present to the God who is always present to you. Call to mind his loving care for you and spend the first minute of your prayer just resting in the free, unearned gift of loving and being loved. Let gratitude rise in your heart.

Lectio: Ask God for the grace to welcome Jesus into your home and to follow him more faithfully in the new year. We will spend this week with selections from the Letter to the Hebrews, which are used as the first readings for the daily Masses in the first week of Ordinary Time. This book of the Bible is often included among the letters of Saint Paul, though it says nothing about who wrote it nor to whom it was written. It makes an extended argument that Jesus is the true High Priest of the new and eternal covenant, which replaces the covenant that God made with the Israelites on Mount Sinai. Because we have a perfect priest, we can have confidence in receiving forgiveness of sins and a path into heaven. Read this passage slowly and prayerfully. Notice whatever stands out to you.

HEBREWS 2:5–12 (LECTIONARY)
It was not to angels that God subjected the world to come,
of which we are speaking.
Instead, someone has testified somewhere:

"What is man that you are mindful of him,
or the son of man that you care for him?
You made him for a little while lower than the angels;
you crowned him with glory and honor,
subjecting all things under his feet."

In "subjecting" all things to him,
he left nothing not "subject to him."

*Yet at present we do not see "all things subject to him,"
but we do see Jesus "crowned with glory and honor"
because he suffered death,
he who "for a little while" was made "lower than the angels," that by the grace of God he might taste death for everyone.*

*For it was fitting that he,
for whom and through whom all things exist,
in bringing many children to glory,
should make the leader to their salvation perfect through
   suffering.
He who consecrates
and those who are being consecrated all have one origin.
Therefore, he is not ashamed to call them "brothers," saying:*

I will proclaim your name to my brethren,
in the midst of the assembly I will praise you.

Meditatio: The author of this letter wants to encourage you to live your Christian life to the full. Do you find yourself sometimes doubting that Jesus is the king of kings and that all power in heaven and on earth has been given to him? Do you sometimes wonder if the Christian life is truly worth living? Jesus is not ashamed to be our brother; are we ashamed to admit to family and friends that we follow him? Read the passage a second time.

Oratio: The one who was "crowned with glory and honor" stands with you in your prayer time. Turn to him. Thank him for tasting death for you and for everyone. Speak to him whatever is on your heart.

Contemplatio: Read the passage a third time. Receive whatever is in Jesus' heart for you. Though he is higher than the angels and all things are subject to him, he cherishes your friendship. Rest in his loving care for you for a little while before moving on.

SUGGESTIONS FOR JOURNALING

1. God feels distant when …
2. I have been burdened by …
3. I sensed Jesus was encouraging me with a reminder that …
4. I ended prayer strengthened by …
5. My prayer today gave me a new insight into how I should think, respond, or act …

_____

_____

_____

_____

_____

_____

_____

_____

_____

_____

_____

_____

_____

_____

_____

_____

_____

_____

After you've journaled, close with a brief conversation thanking Jesus for being your savior and for meeting you in your prayer time today. Then pray an Our Father.

Wednesday of the First Week in Ordinary Time

Preparation: *Come, Holy Spirit, enlighten the eyes of my heart.* Be present to the God who is always present to you. Call to mind his loving care for you and spend the first minute of your prayer just resting in the free, unearned gift of loving and being loved. Let gratitude rise in your heart.

Lectio: Ask God for the grace to see your Savior in a new light, and to accept Jesus' offer to expiate your sins. In former ages, the inevitability of death was unavoidable. The Romans often had themselves buried along roadways so they would be remembered. Travelers couldn't help but notice the dead. A popular epitaph said, "What you are, I once was. What I am, you will be." Romans would gather in cemeteries for picnics with their deceased loved ones. Frequent plagues, natural disasters, and tragic accidents often reminded people that they were living under a sentence of death, and they had very little control over when they passed. When tyrants want to control people, they threaten them with death. Modern American life has banished death to the periphery. The cemetery is not a common destination until your own parents are buried there. We often think of our own death as years in the future. Families are increasingly choosing not to have any service at all and not even to bury their deceased relatives. Yet, you can only avoid death for so long. As you read this passage, picture your own headstone. At that point, there will be only one who can help you.

HEBREWS 2:14–18 (LECTIONARY)

Since the children share in blood and Flesh,
Jesus likewise shared in them,
that through death he might destroy the one
who has the power of death, that is, the Devil,
and free those who through fear of death
had been subject to slavery all their life.

Surely he did not help angels
but rather the descendants of Abraham;
therefore, he had to become like his brothers in every
way, that he might be a merciful and faithful high priest
*   before God*
to expiate the sins of the people.
Because he himself was tested through what he suffered,
he is able to help those who are being tested.

Meditatio: We don't often think of Jesus as being tested by his earthly life. We tend to think more commonly that he sailed through life with no worries at all. But the Bible tells a different story. It depicts Jesus as being tempted, weeping at the death of loved ones (see Jn 11:35), and so much afraid of suffering that he sweated drops of blood (Lk 22:44). His suffering was for you, so that he could help you in your suffering. Read the passage a second time with a sense of gratitude for what Jesus did for you.

Oratio: The one who became like his brothers in every way is with you in your prayer time today. Talk to Jesus about what you are suffering, about the tests you are enduring, about the fear of death and the slavery of everyday life that you are experiencing. Speak to him whatever is on your heart.

Contemplatio: Read the passage a third time. Receive whatever is in Jesus' heart for you. He who shared in flesh and blood knows what you are going through. Receive his care for you. Cherish his friendship and his loving presence with you for a few minutes.

SUGGESTIONS FOR JOURNALING

1. One way that Jesus is like me is …
2. I have experienced the fear of death when …
3. I experienced freedom from fear and hope in Jesus Christ when …
4. I ended prayer strengthened by …
5. My prayer today gave me a new insight into how I should think, respond, or act …

After you've journaled, close with a brief conversation thanking Jesus for being with you in your prayer time today. Then pray an Our Father.

Thursday of the First Week in Ordinary Time

Preparation: *Come, Holy Spirit, enlighten the eyes of my heart.* Be present to the God who is always present to you. Call to mind his loving care for you and spend the first minute of your prayer just resting in the free, unearned gift of loving and being loved. Let gratitude rise in your heart.

Lectio: Ask God for the grace to welcome Jesus into your life and to follow him more faithfully in the new year. The bulk of today's reading is a quote from Psalm 95. The psalm is referring to an episode from Exodus when the Israelites doubted God. They wandered for forty years until the doubters had died; the next generation had more trust in God and was able to enter the promised land. The author of the Letter to the Hebrews is concerned that a similar fate might befall Christians. He doesn't want those of us who have experienced God's power and love to become discouraged and unfaithful to the Gospel. As you read the passage, sense the love that is behind this warning.

HEBREWS 3:7–14 (LECTIONARY)
The Holy Spirit says:
Oh, that today you would hear his voice,
"Harden not your hearts as at the rebellion
in the day of testing in the desert,
where your ancestors tested and tried me
and saw my works for forty years.
Because of this I was provoked with that generation
and I said, 'They have always been of erring heart,
and they do not know my ways.'
As I swore in my wrath,
'They shall not enter into my rest.'"
Take care, brothers and sisters,

that none of you may have an evil and unfaithful heart,
so as to forsake the living God.
Encourage yourselves daily while it is still "today,"
so that none of you may grow hardened by the deceit of
sin. We have become partners of Christ
if only we hold the beginning of the reality firm until the end.

Meditatio: Yesterday we read how Jesus was tempted and tested. We can expect nothing less for ourselves. Have we become discouraged by our wandering in the desert, the depths of winter, or the deceitful hearts of others? Recall the good things God has done for you and how he has invited you to be a partner of Christ in his mission of saving the world. Read the passage a second time.

Oratio: Have you fallen into the deceit of sin? Justifying ourselves, or hiding our faults from God, is a sure path to an evil and unfaithful heart. Today is the time to act. Be completely honest with the Lord, who loves you and walks with you on your journey into his rest. Speak to him whatever is on your heart.

Contemplatio: Read the passage a third time. We don't have to wait until our life is over to enjoy the peace and rest of God's kingdom. It is, in fact, God's desire to bring heaven right into your heart. Wherever you are right now, physically and spiritually speaking, the door is open for you to enter into God's rest. Open now the door of your heart to communion with God. Receive what he wants to give you and rest in his loving presence for a few minutes.

SUGGESTIONS FOR JOURNALING

1. Have I hardened my heart against what the voice of God might say to me — what God might call me to, how he might challenge me, or what he might ask of me?
2. I wandered in the desert when ...
3. In today's prayer time I felt encouraged that ...
4. My heart rested when ...
5. I ended prayer strengthened by ...

_____

_____

_____

_____

_____

_____

_____

_____

_____

_____

_____

_____

_____

_____

_____

_____

_____

_____

After you've journaled, close with a brief conversation thanking Jesus for being with you in your prayer time today. Then pray an Our Father.

January 13 — Friday
Friday of the First Week in Ordinary Time

Preparation: *Come, Holy Spirit, enlighten the eyes of my heart.* Be present to the God who is always present to you. Call to mind his loving care for you and spend the first minute of your prayer just resting in the free, unearned gift of loving and being loved. Let gratitude rise in your heart.

Lectio: Ask God for the grace to follow Jesus more faithfully in the new year and to enter into God's rest now and in eternity. What does God's "rest" mean? Genesis 1 tells us that God created the world in six days and then rested on the seventh. The seventh day was thus blessed as a "day of rest." The third commandment reminds us to keep holy this sabbath day of rest. The promised land was a "place of rest" that awaited Israel at the end of their forty years of wandering in the desert (see Ps 95:11 and Dt 12:9). The author of Hebrews sees our journey on earth like a wandering desert, with the sabbath rest of the heavenly kingdom awaiting us at the end. What do we have to do in order to enter into God's eternal rest? Let's find out. Read the passage slowly and prayerfully.

HEBREWS 4:1–5, 11 (LECTIONARY)
Let us be on our guard
while the promise of entering into his rest remains,
that none of you seem to have failed.
For in fact we have received the Good News just as our
      ancestors did.
But the word that they heard did not profit them,
for they were not united in faith with those who listened.
For we who believed enter into that rest,
just as he has said:

As I swore in my wrath,
"They shall not enter into my rest,"

and yet his works were accomplished
at the foundation of the world.
For he has spoken somewhere about the seventh day in
*   this manner,*
And God rested on the seventh day from all his works;
and again, in the previously mentioned place,
They shall not enter into my rest.

Therefore, let us strive to enter into that rest,
so that no one may fall after the same example of
*   disobedience.*

Meditatio: I see three things required of us in today's reading: faith, belief, and obedience. The Bible presents faith in the context of relationship. Having faith in God is similar to the kind of faith I would put in a friend, or the experience of a husband and wife who have been faithful to each other for forty years. Over the years of wandering and testing, God has always been faithful to me. I believe that he will be faithful to the end. My belief then becomes "incarnate" in the daily choices of my everyday life, my obedience to God's law and my faithfulness to his commands. Do you believe in God's faithfulness? Are you faithful to God by your daily obedience? Read the passage a second time. Notice whatever word or phrase speaks to you.

Oratio: We often talk about blind faith, and we know that God sometimes invites us to take a step into darkness. However, my experience is that God will earn your trust. He invites you to take a step in faith. When you say "Yes" you experience the fact that God knew what was best for you. As we trust God more often and more regularly, we build up faith, and we see that God is trustworthy. Do you feel God inviting you to something difficult? Do you struggle to trust in him? Why not talk to God about that right now.

Contemplatio: Read the passage a third time. Faith in God allows us to let go of the need to know everything and to be in control. We can rest in his divine providence and his loving care for us. We don't have to wait until heaven to enter into God's rest; experience his rest right now by resting in his loving care for you.

SUGGESTIONS FOR JOURNALING

1. Am I a naturally trusting person, or a person who is naturally skeptical and suspicious? Do I struggle with "trust issues"?
2. When did I trust in God and it turned out to be a good thing?
3. Were there times when I trusted in God, and he seemed to disappoint me and let me down? Have I talked to him about that experience?
4. My heart rested when …
5. I ended prayer with a deeper sense that …

_____

_____

_____

_____

_____

_____

_____

_____

_____

_____

_____

_____

_____

_____

_____

_____

_____

_____

_____

_____

_____

After you've journaled, close with a brief conversation thanking God for his faithfulness to you and his patience with you in your prayer time today. Then pray an Our Father.

January 14 — Saturday
Saturday of the First Week in Ordinary Time

REVIEW

Preparation: *Come, Holy Spirit, enlighten the eyes of my heart.* Call to mind his loving care for you and spend the first minute of your prayer just resting in the free, unearned gift of loving and being loved. Let gratitude rise in your heart.

We have just spent a week with the Letter to the Hebrews. The author wants to make sure that Christians who once experienced God's loving care are not discouraged by their sinfulness or the unfaithfulness of others. How have we experienced God's loving care for you this past week? Here are some questions to help you:

1. Where did I notice God, and what was he doing or saying?
2. How did I respond to what God was doing?
3. I felt God's love most strongly when …
4. I found myself struggling with …
5. I'm grateful for …
6. This past week, my strongest sense, image, moment, or experience of God's loving presence was …

Conclude by conversing with God about your week. **Acknowledge** what you have been experiencing. **Relate** it to him. **Receive** what he wants to give you. **Respond** to him. Then savor that image of God's loving presence and rest there for a minute or two. Close with an Our Father.

Week Eight

Discernment of Spirits

"How do I know it's really God that is speaking to me?"

St. Ignatius of Loyola was a master of the discernment of spirits. He distinguishes between the spirit of God and the enemy. He says that if we are generally living for ourselves and engaging in mortal sin, the enemy spirit will try to keep us lulled into a false sense of security and comfort. For example, "Just a quick look at porn never hurt anyone." Or, "You can quit drinking tomorrow. Tonight, enjoy yourself." For this kind of person, the work of the Good Spirit will feel like a slap in the face or an alarm clock (some people use the expression "spiritual 2x4") because the Good Spirit has to shake us out of our stupor so that we can see the danger to our soul.

On the other hand, for a person who is generally growing in faith, living for God, and trying to avoid sin, the work of the two spirits is the opposite. The enemy wants us to stop growing, so he will propose imaginary obstacles, discouragements, distractions, and confusion. Sometimes the enemy will try to convince you that you aren't holy enough and you need to do so much more for God. The voice of the enemy will be accusatory ("You're not good enough"; "You're broken"; "No one could love someone like you"; "You're doing it wrong; everyone else is having a better retreat than you"; "You missed a few days, you might as well quit, you could try again next year …";). These thoughts come with feelings of unrest, fear, sometimes panic. The Good Spirit, on the other hand, will be encouraging and supportive and come with a sense of peace. The spirit will remind us that we are loved, valued, and forgiven. Even when we need a "wake-up call," it will feel more like a gentle nudge.

Ignatius warned us that spiritual people will tend to go through periods of consolation and desolation. Consolation is when we can feel God's love and have a sense of peace and his presence; the right choices are obvious. Desolation is when we can't feel God's love, and instead we hear the voice of the enemy more strongly; right seems wrong, and bad choices come easily. Think of consolation like a sunny day and desolation like a dark and stormy night. In desolation, we should not make a change, but keep walking on the road that we saw clearly when we were in consolation. In consolation, we should draw strength from God's love and prepare ourselves for when desolation comes again.

This pattern of easy and difficult, comfort and struggle, is to be expected on pilgrimages. Some days we feel strong and comforted, and we make progress easily. Other days are windy, cold, exhausting, and we find we have to put our heads down and just focus on putting one blistered foot in front of the other. The difficult times test your mettle and force you to face your fears and burdens. The times of resistance are actually the times of the most spiritual growth. So do not be discouraged if you have faced resistance, difficulties praying each day, and lots of struggles from inside of you and from outside. Resistance is a sign that you are on the right road and that, by overcoming obstacles, spiritual progress is happening. The only way to have a "bad pilgrimage" is to quit. Just keep walking, however slowly it may be, and you will eventually reach your goal.

Grace of the Week: Inspired by Sunday's reading from the Prophet Isaiah, we will depart from the daily Mass readings to spend three days with the Prophet Isaiah and three days with Saint Luke. This may be the most powerful week of the whole pilgrimage. Pray for your fellow pilgrims and know that I am praying for you. Ask God for the grace to receive and live your true identity in Christ.

January 15 — Sunday
Second Sunday in Ordinary Time

Preparation: *Come, Holy Spirit, enlighten the eyes of my heart.* Be present to the God who is always present to you. Call to mind his loving care for you and spend the first minute of your prayer just resting in the free, unearned gift of loving and being loved. Let gratitude rise in your heart.

Lectio: Ask God for the grace to receive and live your true identity in Christ. Today we will meditate on the extended version of the first reading from the lectionary. This is one of four passages from Isaiah that refer to a mysterious Servant of the Lord (see Is 42:1–9; 49:1–7; 50:4–9; and 52:13—53:12). The servant is identified as "Israel" (which could refer to the whole people), who by doing God's work shows forth his glory. But then later on in the passage, the servant is identified as one who brings back Jacob and restores Israel (Jacob and Israel are two names for the same person, the grandson of Abraham and the father of the "twelve tribes of Israel"). Who is this mysterious figure? Read the passage slowly and prayerfully.

ISAIAH 49:1–6
Hear me, coastlands,
listen, distant peoples.
Before birth the Lord called me,
from my mother's womb he gave me my name.
He made my mouth like a sharp-edged sword,
concealed me, shielded by his hand.
He made me a sharpened arrow,
in his quiver he hid me.
He said to me, You are my servant,
in you, Israel, I show my glory.

Though I thought I had toiled in vain,

> *for nothing and for naught spent my strength,*
> Yet my right is with the LORD,
>   *my recompense is with my God.*
> For now the LORD has spoken
>   *who formed me as his servant from the womb,*
> That Jacob may be brought back to him
>   *and Israel gathered to him;*
> I am honored in the sight of the LORD,
>   *and my God is now my strength!*
> It is too little, he says, for you to be my servant,
>   *to raise up the tribes of Jacob,*
>   *and restore the survivors of Israel;*
> I will make you a light to the nations,
>   *that my salvation may reach to the ends of the earth.*

Meditatio: Early Christians recognized in Isaiah's mysterious Servant of the Lord prophecies referring to Jesus Christ. Jesus saves the people, and in doing so becomes the leader of God's holy people, the Church. We are each called to not only receive salvation from Christ, but also to show God's glory by our faithful service to the King. What does this passage say about Jesus the Servant of the Lord? How does this passage call me to be a more faithful servant of the Lord? Notice whatever word or phrase stands out to you as you read the passage a second time.

Oratio: God formed you in the womb and knew your name before you were born. He has been sharpening you for your special mission, concealing you in his quiver. How did Jesus prepare for his mission? How are you called to participate in Jesus' mission of salvation? What special gift, blessing, or task has God assigned to you? Ask God these questions. If you find yourself afraid, feeling like you have spent your strength for nothing, or convinced that you couldn't possibly have a special mission, talk to God about that as well. Be open and honest with him.

Contemplatio: Read the passage a third time. This time just receive whatever God wants to give you. Perhaps he will invite you to a new way of seeing, thinking, or believing. Perhaps he will remind you of a past prayer time, experience, or encounter that speaks of your mission and purpose. Be open to receive whatever God wants to give you. Sometimes our own goodness is the hardest thing to believe in. Be with the Lord who loves you, and enjoy this time together. Savor his presence for a minute or two before moving on.

SUGGESTIONS FOR JOURNALING

1. The part of the prophecy that most spoke to me was …
2. My strongest thought, feeling, or desire was …
3. I have a hard time believing that …
4. I noticed God's presence most strongly …
5. What part do I play in bringing God's salvation to the ends of the earth?

After you've journaled, close with a brief conversation giving thanks to God for your prayer experience. Then pray an Our Father.

Monday of the Second Week in Ordinary Time

Preparation: *Come, Holy Spirit, enlighten the eyes of my heart.* Be present to the God who is always present to you. Call to mind his loving care for you and spend the first minute of your prayer just resting in the free, unearned gift of loving and being loved. Let gratitude rise in your heart.

Lectio: Ask God for the grace to receive and live your true identity in Christ. We pick up where we left off with yesterday's selection from Isaiah. We can see God lifting up the lowly and bringing down the mighty. We can see his great pity for his holy people, the prisoners, and those in darkness. Picture the Good News and the return from exile as you read the passage slowly and prayerfully.

ISAIAH 49:7–12

Thus says the LORD,
　　the redeemer, the Holy One of Israel,
To the one despised, abhorred by the nations,
　　the slave of rulers:
When kings see you, they shall stand up,
　　and princes shall bow down
Because of the LORD who is faithful,
　　the Holy One of Israel who has chosen you.

　　Thus says the LORD:
In a time of favor I answer you,
　　on the day of salvation I help you;
I form you and set you
　　as a covenant for the people,
To restore the land
　　and allot the devastated heritages,
To say to the prisoners: Come out!

> *To those in darkness: Show yourselves!*
> *Along the roadways they shall find pasture,*
>   *on every barren height shall their pastures be.*
> *They shall not hunger or thirst;*
>   *nor shall scorching wind or sun strike them;*
> *For he who pities them leads them*
>   *and guides them beside springs of water.*
> *I will turn all my mountains into roadway,*
>   *and make my highways level.*
> *See, these shall come from afar:*
>   *some from the north and the west,*
>   *others from the land of Syene.*

Meditatio: In its original context, this passage is an oracle of encouragement to the nation of Israel that is now living in exile in Babylon. They are longing to return to their own homeland. The "slave of rulers" could also refer to Israel enslaved in Egypt and the trip to the promised land. But more to our point today, the passage could also refer to all God's children, faithful Christians who feel oppressed; some are literally in prison right now for their belief in Jesus. They shall all be brought home safely to the kingdom of heaven. Notice the thoughts, feelings, and desires that stir in you as you read this passage a second time.

Oratio: Are you grateful that God has been faithful to you? Do you have confidence in his plan to bring you out of darkness and to free you from the prison of sin and death? Are you longing for a true homeland, a "place of rest"? What do you hunger and thirst for? Share with God the thoughts, feelings, and desires that well up within you.

Contemplatio: Read the passage a third time. This time just receive whatever God wants to give you. Be assured of his loving presence with you, his loving care for you, and his beautiful plan to save you. Rest for a few minutes in whatever way he reveals his presence to you in your prayer time today.

SUGGESTIONS FOR JOURNALING

1. In today's reading, I could most identify myself with …
2. My strongest thought, feeling, or desire was …
3. I hunger and thirst for …
4. God was with me, and he wanted me to know …
5. What part can I play in helping the other exiles find their way home to God?

After you've journaled, close with a brief conversation giving thanks to God for his presence with you in prayer today. Then pray an Our Father.

January 17 — Tuesday
Tuesday of the Second Week in Ordinary Time

SAINT ANTHONY, ABBOT

Anthony was born in Egypt around AD 251. At the age of eighteen or so, he was in a church and heard the Bible passage, "Go, sell what you have, and give to the poor, and you will have treasure in heaven; then come, follow me" (Mk 10:21). He believed this was a personal invitation from God directed to him. He gave away his earthly possessions and went out into the desert to live a simple life of prayer and penance. During this period, the Church transitioned from a persecuted minority to a kind of state religion. Christianity became too easy and comfortable for many, who desired to give their all for Jesus. So, they went out into the desert and joined Anthony. He wrote a rule for them, which became the foundations of the monastic life.

Preparation: *Come, Holy Spirit, enlighten the eyes of my heart.* Be present to the God who is always present to you. Call to mind his loving care for you and spend the first minute of your prayer just resting in the free, unearned gift of loving and being loved. Let gratitude rise in your heart.

Lectio: Ask God for the grace to receive and live your true identity in Christ. Do you ever feel like God has forsaken you? You are not alone! I daresay every Christian, and even Christ himself, has felt like this at some time or another. Today's passage picks up where Monday's ended. Zion is the name of the hill on which the city of Jerusalem is built, and it is used to refer to the city and, consequently, also to the people. God gives his people three separate images of how much they can depend on his love. Which of the images most speaks to you? Read the passage slowly and prayerfully.

ISAIAH 49:13–16

> *Sing out, heavens, and rejoice, earth,*
> *break forth into song, you mountains,*

For the LORD comforts his people
and shows mercy to his afflicted.

But Zion said, "The LORD has forsaken me;
my Lord has forgotten me."
Can a mother forget her infant,
be without tenderness for the child of her womb?
Even should she forget,
I will never forget you.
See, upon the palms of my hands I have engraved you;
your walls are ever before me.

Meditatio: The Jewish people are living in exile in a foreign land. They feel forgotten by God. They must be patient until God is ready to allow them to return. Trusting in God and waiting for him do not come easily. Would a mother ever forget her child? God's love is greater than that. Can you believe that God has not forgotten you? Look at your own hands. Can you picture your name carved into the palm of God's hand? It's like when we write a note on our hand so we won't forget something; God has written your name right where he can see it. When he looks up, he sees the walls of your home. Meditate on these visual reminders. Notice the thoughts, feelings, and desires that stir in you as you read this passage a second time.

Oratio: I often feel God's loving presence with me during my prayer times. The rest of the day God seems to be distant from me. The truth is, God didn't go anywhere. God is always present to me and with me, but I am only sometimes open to that loving presence. Are you waiting for some feeling or change in circumstances to assure you of God's love for you? His comfort and mercy are available right now; all you have to do is ask! Speak to God from the longing you have to be seen and known and comforted. Speak to him with gratitude that you are a beloved child and your name is carved on his palms.

Contemplatio: Read the passage a third time. This time just receive whatever God wants to give you. Rest for a few minutes with confidence in his unshakable love for you.

SUGGESTIONS FOR JOURNALING

1. I sometimes doubt God's love for me because …
2. The word, phrase, or image that most spoke to me was …
3. A fear that surfaced during today's prayer time is the thought that …
4. I find myself longing for …
5. God wanted to remind me …
6. What part can I play in helping remind others of God's unshakable love for them?

After you've journaled, close with a brief conversation giving thanks to God for his presence with you in prayer today. Then pray an Our Father.

January 18 — Wednesday

Wednesday of the Second Week in Ordinary Time

Preparation: *Come, Holy Spirit, enlighten the eyes of my heart.* Be present to the God who is always present to you. Call to mind his loving care for you and spend the first minute of your prayer just resting in the free, unearned gift of loving and being loved. Let gratitude rise in your heart.

Set the Scene: Ask God for the grace to receive your identity as a beloved child of God, loved unconditionally by your Father. No doubt, you are familiar with today's passage. Ask for the grace to see it with fresh eyes. Read the passage and picture the story in vivid detail — the beautiful estate of the father, the stink of the pigsty, the filth still clinging to the son's tattered clothes when he finally arrives home again.

LUKE 15:11–24

Then he said, "A man had two sons, and the younger son said to his father, 'Father, give me the share of your estate that should come to me.' So the father divided the property between them. After a few days, the younger son collected all his belongings and set off to a distant country where he squandered his inheritance on a life of dissipation. When he had freely spent everything, a severe famine struck that country, and he found himself in dire need. So he hired himself out to one of the local citizens who sent him to his farm to tend the swine. And he longed to eat his fill of the pods on which the swine fed, but nobody gave him any. Coming to his senses he thought, 'How many of my father's hired workers have more than enough food to eat, but here am I, dying from hunger. I shall get up and go to my father and I shall say to him, "Father, I have sinned against heaven and against you. I no longer deserve to be called your son; treat me as you would treat one of your hired workers."' So he got up and went back to his father. While he was still a long way off, his father caught sight of him, and was filled with compassion. He ran to his son, embraced him and kissed him. His son said to him, 'Father, I have sinned against heaven and against you; I no longer deserve to be called your son.' But his father ordered his servants, 'Quickly bring the finest robe and put it on him; put a ring on his finger and sandals on his feet. Take the fattened calf and slaughter it. Then let us celebrate with a feast, because this son of mine was dead, and has come to life again; he was lost, and has been found.' Then the celebration began.

Action! You might think that God can't, won't, or shouldn't forgive you. This son basically told his father, "I'm sick of waiting for you to die. Give me my inheritance now." Then he went and blew it all. His miserable state is a natural result of breaking off the relationship with his father. When the son does decide to go home, it's not because he misses his father or wants to restore the relationship; he is looking for a job. What father would welcome such a miserable son back to his home? How would you have expected the story to end? Jesus wants his hearers to realize that God the Father is unbelievably patient and merciful. Picture yourself as the prodigal son. Feel the hunger, the long journey home. Feel the father's embrace and kiss. The robe, ring, and sandals show your sonship. What thoughts and feelings rise inside of you? Read the passage a second time.

Acknowledge: What thought, feeling, or desire was most prominent? Is there something underneath those feelings that also needs to be talked about?

Relate: Picture the Father embracing you, or sit with him after the party. Tell him what is on your heart. There's no reason to hide anything from your Father. Be completely honest with him, maybe for the first time in your life.

Receive: Read the passage a third time, or just the part that most speaks to you. Look at the Father, and let him look at you. Receive what is in his heart for you — his love, patience, kindness, and mercy.

Respond: Can you accept his love for you? Perhaps you need to give God permission to love you. Of course it is undeserved! None of us deserves a Father like this. Perhaps you believe the lie that you're broken beyond repair. What lies keep you from accepting the Father's love for you? Face them. Talk about them. Let the Father tell you the truth. Receive his love for you and then rest in that loving embrace for a little while.

SUGGESTIONS FOR JOURNALING

1. When and why have I felt unworthy of the Father's love for me? Have I behaved in ways unbecoming of a son or daughter of God?
2. When I think of the Father's unconditional love, I'm reminded of the time that (some experience in your life) …
3. The Father wanted me to know …
4. In the name of Jesus, I reject the lie that … (Say it three times.)
5. In the name of Jesus, I accept the truth that … (Say it three times.)
6. In what area of my life am I called to love others as the Father has loved me?

_____
_____
_____
_____
_____
_____
_____
_____
_____
_____
_____
_____
_____
_____
_____
_____
_____
_____
_____
_____

After you've journaled, close with thanksgiving to God the Father, Son, and Holy Spirit for your prayer experience. End with an Our Father.

+

The U.S. bishops' "9 Days for Life" novena begins January 19. Learn more at www.9daysforlife.com.

January 19 — Thursday

Thursday of the Second Week in Ordinary Time

Preparation: *Come, Holy Spirit, enlighten the eyes of my heart.* Be present to the God who is always present to you. Call to mind his loving care for you and spend the first minute of your prayer just resting in the free, unearned gift of loving and being loved. Let gratitude rise in your heart.

Set the Scene: Ask God for the grace to receive your identity as a beloved child of God, loved unconditionally by your Father. The parable of the prodigal son continues. Remember how the man had two sons? The elder son is the faithful, responsible, obedient son. He reacts to his younger brother's return in a very different way. Read the Gospel and picture the story in vivid detail — the beautiful estate of the father, the elder son coming back from a hard day of work in the fields, and the lights and sounds of a party filtering out to greet him.

LUKE 15:25–32

"Now the older son had been out in the field and, on his way back, as he neared the house, he heard the sound of music and dancing. He called one of the servants and asked what this might mean. The servant said to him, 'Your brother has returned and your father has slaughtered the fattened calf because he has him back safe and sound.' He became angry, and when he refused to enter the house, his father came out and pleaded with him. He said to his father in reply, 'Look, all these years I served you and not once did I disobey your orders; yet you never gave me even a young goat to feast on with my friends. But when your son returns who swallowed up your property with prostitutes, for him you slaughter the fattened calf.' He said to him, 'My son, you are here with me always; everything I have is yours. But now we must cele-

brate and rejoice, because your brother was dead and has come to life again; he was lost and has been found.'"

Action! Jesus tells this parable in response to the objection of the scribes and Pharisees that he "welcomes sinners and eats with them" (Lk 15:2). The elder son is meant to symbolize the faithful and righteous people who refuse to rejoice when sinners repent. Devout, faithful Christians often find themselves lamenting how God seems to let others off easy. If you had a hard time yesterday seeing yourself as the prodigal son, you will probably find it much easier to picture yourself as the elder brother. Read the passage a second time.

Acknowledge: What thought, feelings, or desires were welling up inside of you? When has your service to God felt like a long, hard day in the fields? Do you sometimes feel that God barely acknowledges the good work that you are doing? If that's how you feel, don't feel ashamed. Feelings are not good or bad, they are just data points that can give us clues to what is going on inside. Notice what is going on inside of you.

Relate: Picture yourself speaking to your Father. Speak your mind, without fear of offending him, as the older son does. Be completely honest with the Father, maybe for the first time in your life.

Receive: Read the passage a third time, or just the part that most speaks to you. The younger son had no clue how much his father truly loved him. He thought the estate and his inheritance and even a good job were worth more. He finally realizes that his greatest gift was his father's love. The older son has been faithful all these years, but he, too, does not realize how much his father truly loves him. I know many, many Christians who have served God faithfully but have never truly experienced God's love for them. Have you experienced how the Father looks at you with love? Look at the Father, and let him look at you. Receive what is in his heart for you — his love, patience, kindness, and mercy.

Respond: Can you accept his love for you? Perhaps you need to give God permission to love you. Perhaps you believe the lie that love has to be earned; the Father will only love those who are good enough. What lies keep you from accepting the Father's love for you? Face them. Talk about them. Let the Father tell you the truth. Receive his love for you and then rest in that loving embrace for a little while.

SUGGESTIONS FOR JOURNALING

1. When and why have I felt like the older brother?
2. The Father wanted me to know …
3. In the name of Jesus, I reject the lie that … (Say it three times.)
4. In the name of Jesus, I accept the truth that … (Say it three times.)
5. In what area of my life am I called to love others as the Father has loved me?

After you've journaled, close with thanksgiving to God the Father, Son, and Holy Spirit for your prayer experience. End with an Our Father.

Friday of the Second Week in Ordinary Time

Preparation: *Come, Holy Spirit, enlighten the eyes of my heart.* Be present to the God who is always present to you. Call to mind his loving care for you and spend the first minute of your prayer just resting in the free, unearned gift of loving and being loved. Let gratitude rise in your heart.

Set the Scene: Ask God for the grace to receive your identity as a beloved child of God, loved unconditionally by your Father. Today we look at another Gospel passage that captures the merciful love of God. Jesus was arrested last night in the Garden of Gethsemane. Under cover of darkness, he was tried and convicted of blasphemy. Scourged and crowned with thorns, he just finished carrying his cross through the streets of Jerusalem and out beyond the walls to the place where criminals are crucified. It's Good Friday afternoon, and Jesus is a laughingstock. Picture the scene as you read this passage.

LUKE 23:33–43

When they came to the place called the Skull, they crucified him and the criminals there, one on his right, the other on his left. [Then Jesus said, "Father, forgive them, they know not what they do."] They divided his garments by casting lots. The people stood by and watched; the rulers, meanwhile, sneered at him and said, "He saved others, let him save himself if he is the chosen one, the Messiah of God." Even the soldiers jeered at him. As they approached to offer him wine they called out, "If you are King of the Jews, save yourself." Above him there was an inscription that read, "This is the King of the Jews."

Now one of the criminals hanging there reviled Jesus, saying, "Are you not the Messiah? Save yourself and us."

> *The other, however, rebuking him, said in reply, "Have you no fear of God, for you are subject to the same condemnation? And indeed, we have been condemned justly, for the sentence we received corresponds to our crimes, but this man has done nothing criminal." Then he said, "Jesus, remember me when you come into your kingdom." He replied to him, "Amen, I say to you, today you will be with me in Paradise."*

Action! What struck you as you read and imagined the scene? Crucifixion was a public event; watching people be crucified was a good reminder to behave. It was a humiliating and excruciating way to die. What is going on in the heart of each person? Jesus has lost everything — his friends deserted him, no one stood up to defend him, even the clothes on his back were taken. He has nothing left but the Father's love. And he is happy to share his Father's love with anyone who will receive it. He forgives his enemies and pardons a guilty thief. What is happening in the heart of Jesus? Read the passage a second time.

Acknowledge: Place yourself in the scene. Where are you? What are you feeling and thinking?

Relate: Turn to Jesus. Speak to him from your heart.

Receive: Read the passage a third time. What is in Jesus' heart for you? How does he respond to you? What does he want to give you?

Respond: Receive whatever Jesus is offering you. If you were the only person in the world, Jesus would still have suffered all this for you. Cherish his friendship, as he cherishes your friendship. Rest in the love Jesus has for you, the same love with which his Father loves him.

SUGGESTIONS FOR JOURNALING
1. What struck me most from today's prayer time was …
2. I have a hard time believing that …
3. Jesus wanted to give me …

4. I see myself in a new light …
5. Who am I called to forgive as Jesus has forgiven me?

After you've journaled, close with thanksgiving to God, Father, Son, and Holy Spirit, for the gift of today's prayer experience. End with an Our Father.

January 21 — Saturday
Saturday of the Second Week in Ordinary Time

SAINT AGNES, VIRGIN AND MARTYR

Tradition holds that Agnes was a young Roman noblewoman martyred under the Emperor Diocletian around the year 304. She is one of seven women mentioned by name in the Roman Canon of the Mass (Eucharistic Prayer I). Her name comes from the Latin word *agnus* meaning "lamb." She is often depicted holding a lamb in witness to the innocence of her youth and virginity. On this day in Rome, the Holy Father blesses two sheep whose wool will be woven into the pallia worn by archbishops.

REVIEW

Preparation: *Come, Holy Spirit, enlighten the eyes of my heart.* Call to mind God's loving care for you and spend the first minute of your prayer just resting in the free, unearned gift of loving and being loved.

Our Scripture passages this past week gave us some powerful and memorable images of God's unconditional love for his children. Let's review those prayer periods and try to draw out some of the blessings we received. Here are some questions to help you:

1. Where did I notice God, and what was he doing or saying?
2. How did I respond to what God was doing?
3. I felt God's love most strongly when …
4. I found myself struggling with …
5. I'm grateful for …
6. This past week, my strongest sense, image, moment, or experience of God's loving presence was …
7. How do I feel God calling me to a new way of loving, as he has loved me?

Conclude by conversing with God about your week. **Acknowledge** what you have been experiencing. **Relate** it to him. **Receive** what he wants to give you. **Respond** to him. Then savor that image of God's loving presence and rest there for a minute or two. Close with an Our Father.

Week Nine

Relational Prayer (ARRR)

I want to teach you a third prayer form, called relational prayer or "A-R-R-R." You've already seen this prayer form as part of imaginative prayer. Let's review the four steps:

Acknowledge what is going on inside of you — your thoughts, feelings, and desires.

Relate, or share with the Lord what is going on inside of you.

Receive what God wants to give you.

Respond to what the Lord just gave you.

This prayer form can stand on its own as a way of praying with the experiences of everyday life. Let's say I'm on the phone with a relative who is upset that my family's plans for Christmas don't fit her expectations. She implies that, "Some people need to learn to be more flexible; they can't just expect the rest of the world to revolve around them." I get angry and say something like, "Do you have any idea how difficult it is to get all of my family on the same page?" "I'm just saying," she says, "I hope you all have yourselves a nice Christmas." And that's the end of the conversation.

Great. Now I've lost the Christmas spirit, and I'm going to be angry the rest of the day. "Does she have any idea how hard I work to make everyone happy, and no one's ever happy ..." I could stew on it, or I could let God help me. So, I go sit in my prayer corner, or just focus on God wherever I happen to be. I start, as we always do, "*Come Holy Spirit, enlighten the eyes of my heart ...*" I call to mind God's loving care for me that I experienced in a recent prayer time and let gratitude rise in my heart. I'm still feeling angry, but I know I'm not alone. Next, I **Acknowledge** what is going on inside of me. Why am I angry? I notice the feelings that happened before I got angry, such as feeling unappreciated or disrespected or not valued. I might realize I have a wound in this area that makes these kinds of conversations hurt more than they should.

Now I turn to Jesus and focus on him. I could also speak to God the Father, the Holy Spirit, or Mother Mary. It might help to call to mind a favorite image, such as the Good Shepherd or Divine Mercy or one of the memorable moments when Jesus and I connected through imaginative prayer. I **Relate** what I'm feeling and share my heart with him. The important thing here is that my focus needs to shift from me and my problem to the Lord. First it was me looking at my problem, then both of us looking at my problem, and now I'm looking at him. I **Receive** what he wants to give me: a feeling, a thought, a reminder, a Scripture passage, etc. I also might realize things about myself. Perhaps I tend to be a pleaser, or I was already frustrated by something else before the conversation even started. I **Respond** by acting out of this new vision by letting go of something, or resolving to handle things differently next time with Jesus' help. I might need to pray for her or forgive her. I might need to forgive myself. I end with gratitude to God.

Try it for yourself at some point this week. You will be surprised how much this simple prayer form will change your life. Sharing your burdens with God makes them shrink like snow in the sunshine.

Grace of the Week: Jesus wants you to come and follow him. What does that mean? We will use Sunday's Gospel as a jumping-off point to explore the call of discipleship in Matthew and Titus and in your own life. **Ask God for the grace to hear Jesus calling you by name and to respond with joy.**

January 22 — Sunday
Third Sunday in Ordinary Time

Preparation: *Come, Holy Spirit, enlighten the eyes of my heart.* Be present to the God who is always present to you. Call to mind his loving care for you and spend the first minute of your prayer just resting in the free, unearned gift of loving and being loved. Let gratitude rise in your heart.

Set the Scene: Ask God for the grace to hear Jesus calling you by name and to respond with joy. When Joshua led the Israelites into the promised land, each of the twelve tribes (except Levi) were allotted a portion (see Jos 19). The portions that fell to Zebulun and Naphtali were in the north, near the Sea of Galilee. It was here that Jesus began his public ministry with the calling of his first disciples. Picture the freshwater waves lapping up on shore, the sun glinting off the sea as Peter and Andrew are busy fishing. Picture James and John doing the chores that manual labor requires. Use your imagination to picture the scene as you read the passage.

MATTHEW 4:12–23 (LECTIONARY)

When Jesus heard that John had been arrested,
he withdrew to Galilee.
He left Nazareth and went to live in Capernaum by the sea,
in the region of Zebulun and Naphtali,
that what had been said through Isaiah the prophet
might be fulfilled:
Land of Zebulun and land of Naphtali,
the way to the sea, beyond the Jordan,
Galilee of the Gentiles,
the people who sit in darkness have seen a great light,
on those dwelling in a land overshadowed by death
light has arisen.
From that time on, Jesus began to preach and say,

"Repent, for the kingdom of heaven is at hand."

*As he was walking by the Sea of Galilee, he saw two broth-
ers, Simon who is called Peter, and his brother Andrew,
casting a net into the sea; they were fishermen.
He said to them,
"Come after me, and I will make you fishers of men."
At once they left their nets and followed him.
He walked along from there and saw two other brothers,
James, the son of Zebedee, and his brother John.
They were in a boat, with their father Zebedee, mending
    their nets.
He called them, and immediately they left their boat and
    their father
and followed him.
He went around all of Galilee,
teaching in their synagogues, proclaiming the gospel of
    the kingdom,
and curing every disease and illness among the people.*

Action! What was going on in the hearts of the four as they heard Jesus calling them? Why did they follow Jesus? What was it like to follow Jesus from synagogue to synagogue and watch him teach and cure and heal? What questions arose in their hearts? What questions arise in your heart? Read the passage a second time.

Acknowledge: Have you heard Jesus calling you by name on your *Oriens* pilgrimage? What did it feel like? Picture Jesus stopping at your place of work and calling you to follow him. What would you think, feel, or desire?

Relate: Do you feel anxious, excited, or afraid? Talk to Jesus about the call. Share with him your questions or concerns. How does he respond to you? Read the passage a third time.

Receive: What is in Jesus' heart for you? Can you see the tenderness, patience, and love with which he responds to your worries and concerns?

Respond: Jesus is obviously inviting you to say yes. But maybe you aren't ready yet, and he respects your freedom. Respond in whatever way you can right now. Ultimately the call is not so much to go somewhere or to do something, but to be with someone who loves you and desires to lead you on the path of life. Be with that someone for a few minutes right now.

SUGGESTIONS FOR JOURNALING

1. As I imagined the scene, what stood out to me was …
2. The call of Jesus feels like …
3. I found myself wondering …
4. To me, following Jesus means that …
5. I end prayer with a sense that …

After you've journaled, close with a brief conversation thanking Jesus for spending this quality time with you. Then pray an Our Father.

January 23 — Monday

Monday of the Third Week in Ordinary Time

DAY OF PRAYER FOR THE LEGAL PROTECTION OF UNBORN CHILDREN (USA)

In the United States of America, January 22 shall be observed as a particular day of penance for violations to the dignity of the human person committed through acts of abortion, and of prayer for the full restoration of the legal guarantee to the right to life. This day is transferred to January 23 when January 22 falls on a Sunday. Do some extra prayer or penance today.

Preparation: *Come, Holy Spirit, enlighten the eyes of my heart.* Be present to the God who is always present to you. Call to mind his loving care for you and spend the first minute of your prayer just resting in the free, unearned gift of loving and being loved. Let gratitude rise in your heart.

Lectio: Ask God for the grace to hear Jesus calling you by name and to respond with joy. The call to follow Jesus is not fundamentally a call to go somewhere or do something. It is a call to *be with Jesus* and to *learn from him.* The first thing we learn from being with Jesus is his absolute trust in, and dependence on, his Father in heaven. Jesus wants us to share his faith. Read the passage slowly and prayerfully. Notice what speaks to your heart, and notice your feelings as you read these words.

MATTHEW 6:24–34

"No one can serve two masters. He will either hate one and love the other, or be devoted to one and despise the other. You cannot serve God and mammon.

"Therefore I tell you, do not worry about your life, what you will eat [or drink], or about your body, what you will wear. Is not life more than food and the body more than

clothing? Look at the birds in the sky; they do not sow or reap, they gather nothing into barns, yet your heavenly Father feeds them. Are not you more important than they? Can any of you by worrying add a single moment to your life-span? Why are you anxious about clothes? Learn from the way the wild flowers grow. They do not work or spin. But I tell you that not even Solomon in all his splendor was clothed like one of them. If God so clothes the grass of the field, which grows today and is thrown into the oven tomorrow, will he not much more provide for you, O you of little faith? So do not worry and say, 'What are we to eat?' or 'What are we to drink?' or 'What are we to wear?' All these things the pagans seek. Your heavenly Father knows that you need them all. But seek first the kingdom [of God] and his righteousness, and all these things will be given you besides. Do not worry about to-morrow; tomorrow will take care of itself. Sufficient for a day is its own evil."

Meditatio: Does this passage seem too good to be true? On my thirty-day silent retreat, I forgot to bring a backpack and had to carry my Bible, journal, and spiritual reading in a plastic grocery bag. I prayed with this passage, and I heard it as a personal invitation to trust the Father. Still, I pointed out to my spiritual director that it wasn't like a book bag would fall from the sky. That afternoon I walked to Goodwill and purchased a nice little book bag at a discount price. The next morning, I stepped out of my dorm room and there, sitting right in front of my door, was a brand-new backpack, so new that it still had the tags on it. A note from a fellow retreatant said he noticed me carrying my books in a grocery bag, and he had this backpack he didn't need. I left my Goodwill book bag in the floor lounge, and another retreatant discovered it as an answer to his prayers. Do we think God is not powerful enough to provide for us? Do you think you are not important enough for God to pay attention to your needs? Or have you gotten in the habit of giving yourself the credit when God answers your prayers? Ponder these questions, then read the passage a second time, slowly and prayerfully.

Oratio: Was there a time when it seemed like God didn't provide for you — when a prayer went unanswered or a need unfulfilled? Have others let you down, making it easy to believe that God, too, will let you down? Listen to your heart and whatever fears, worries, or hurts are present there. Then speak to God honestly and openly about your concerns.

Contemplatio: Read the passage a third time. This time listen for how God answers your heart. God will earn your trust if you give him the chance. Will you give him the chance today? Spend some time with Jesus and his Father before moving on.

SUGGESTIONS FOR JOURNALING

1. The word, phrase, or idea that most spoke to me from today's passage was …
2. I have experienced God's providence when …
3. I want to trust God, but I am afraid that …
4. Jesus trusted his Father and wants me to do the same. What about the example of Jesus encourages me?
5. God doesn't stop responding just because we end our prayer time. Keep your eyes open for God's providence today and spend some time journaling those moments at the end of today's prayer time or when you pray tomorrow.

_____

_____

_____

_____

_____

_____

_____

_____

_____

_____

_____

_____

_____

_____

_____

_____

_____

_____

After you've journaled, close with a brief conversation thanking God for providing for your needs in today's prayer experience. Then pray an Our Father.

January 24 — Tuesday
Tuesday of the Third Week in Ordinary Time

ST. FRANCIS DE SALES

Born August 21, 1567, Francis was the son of a senator from the province of Savoy in France. His father sent him to study law to follow in his own footsteps. Francis, however, felt a call to become a priest. He patiently and gently won his father's consent. Part of his conversion happened when he heard a Calvinist preach on predestination and became convinced that he was predestined for eternal damnation. Eventually he came to experience God's love for him and realized a loving God would not predestine anyone to hell. He was an effective preacher himself and converted many Calvinists back to the Catholic Faith. At the age of thirty-five, he was named bishop of Geneva, then being run as an autocratic theocracy by none other than John Calvin himself. He spent twenty years conquering his quick temper, so much so that he became famous for his gentle character. His many pamphlets on the Faith, famous books, and exhaustive correspondence made him a patron of the Catholic press.

Preparation: *Come, Holy Spirit, enlighten the eyes of my heart.* Be present to the God who is always present to you. Call to mind his loving care for you and spend the first minute of your prayer just resting in the free, unearned gift of loving and being loved. Let gratitude rise in your heart.

Set the Scene: Ask God for the grace to hear Jesus calling you by name and to respond with joy. At first glance, it appears that Jesus is trying to be alone to mourn the death of his cousin. However, Jesus' actions have symbolic value. Up until this point, he has been traveling from town to town and mostly preaching in synagogues where the people readily gather. By moving to a deserted place, he is inviting them to seek him out. Those who seek him are rewarded. It also creates an opportunity of faith for Jesus' disciples. Will they trust in the Father, as Jesus does? Read the passage and picture the scene in your imagination.

MATTHEW 14:13-21

When Jesus heard of [the death of John the Baptist], he withdrew in a boat to a deserted place by himself. The crowds heard of this and followed him on foot from their towns. When he disembarked and saw the vast crowd, his heart was moved with pity for them, and he cured their sick. When it was evening, the disciples approached him and said, "This is a deserted place and it is already late; dismiss the crowds so that they can go to the villages and buy food for themselves." [Jesus] said to them, "There is no need for them to go away; give them some food yourselves." But they said to him, "Five loaves and two fish are all we have here." Then he said, "Bring them here to me," and he ordered the crowds to sit down on the grass. Taking the five loaves and the two fish, and looking up to heaven, he said the blessing, broke the loaves, and gave them to the disciples, who in turn gave them to the crowds. They all ate and were satisfied, and they picked up the fragments left over — twelve wicker baskets full. Those who ate were about five thousand men, not counting women and children.

Action! When God seems to withdraw, do you make the effort to seek him out? What do you do when your resources appear too small to meet the demands that are placed upon you? I know you've experienced the feeling of not enough time, not enough money, not enough knowledge or skill or talent. If you did some fasting for the unborn yesterday, you might have been reminded of the desperate craving that hunger brings. Jesus shows us what to do when we don't have enough: Take the little that we do have and give it to him. I experienced having not enough time to write this book. I gave it to God, and I had the time I needed to finish, as you can see by the fact that you are holding this book in your hands. What does each person experience in today's reading? Put yourself into the passage wherever you feel most comfortable — as a disciple or as one of the five thousand. Notice your own thoughts and feelings as you read the passage a second time.

Acknowledge: What are the thoughts, feelings, and desires that arise in your heart? What are you hungry for? Where do you feel inadequate?

Relate: Sit with Jesus on the grass and talk to him about it. Everyone else is busy eating or napping after the meal so he has plenty of time to listen just to you.

Receive: Read the passage a third time. How does Jesus respond? What is he inviting you to?

Respond: Childlike trust is possible for all of us. It may look hard, but it's actually easier than the way you are already living your life. We have been taught not to trust and to make life more complicated than it was meant to be. Can you see yourself, and the world, as Jesus sees you? Can you do what Jesus asks you to do? Don't force yourself. Jesus reverences your freedom, and you should too. Enjoy Jesus' patient, gentle, loving presence with you for a few minutes before moving on.

SUGGESTIONS FOR JOURNALING

1. As I imagined the scene, what stood out to me was …
2. When have I felt inadequate?
3. Was there a time when I turned over my inadequacy to Jesus and he blessed me with more than enough?
4. In what area of my life is Jesus inviting me to greater trust?
5. I ended prayer with a sense that …

After you've journaled, close with a brief conversation thanking God for his loving care for you experienced in today's prayer time. Then pray an Our Father.

January 25 — Wednesday

Wednesday of the Third Week in Ordinary Time

THE CONVERSION OF SAINT PAUL, APOSTLE

How did it happen that Saul of Tarsus, zealous Jewish student of the law and persecutor of Christians, became Paul the apostle and died for the Jesus he had once blasphemed? He was present when Stephen was martyred and consented to the stoning (see Acts 7:58, 8:1). Perhaps Stephen loved his enemies and prayed for those who persecuted him. Today we commemorate Saul's conversion, after Jesus appeared to him on the road to Damascus and called his name (Acts 22:3–16). He had a conversion, and went on to become a great missionary of the Gospel in pagan lands. He wrote many of the letters of the New Testament. The site of his burial is now one of the four major basilicas of Rome. Saint Paul gave what he had to Jesus, and Jesus used him to do great things. How is God calling you to put your life in his hands today?

Preparation: *Come, Holy Spirit, enlighten the eyes of my heart.* Be present to the God who is always present to you. Call to mind his loving care for you and spend the first minute of your prayer just resting in the free, unearned gift of loving and being loved. Let gratitude rise in your heart.

Set the Scene: Ask God for the grace to hear Jesus calling you by name and to step out of the boat with faith. The Sea of Galilee is not excessively large. Extending thirteen miles north to south and seven miles east to west, most days an observer on one shore can easily see the opposite shore. Due to the interaction with surrounding arid land and the nearby Mediterranean Sea, violent squalls sometimes blow up. The disciples have literally been rowing all night. We know this because the Romans divided the night into four "watches," equal periods of time between sunset and sunrise. The "fourth watch" is the final three-hour period before sunrise. Read the passage and picture the scene in your imagination.

MATTHEW 14:22–33

> *Then he made the disciples get into the boat and precede him to the other side, while he dismissed the crowds. After doing so, he went up on the mountain by himself to pray. When it was evening he was there alone. Meanwhile the boat, already a few miles offshore, was being tossed about by the waves, for the wind was against it. During the fourth watch of the night, he came toward them, walking on the sea. When the disciples saw him walking on the sea they were terrified. "It is a ghost," they said, and they cried out in fear. At once [Jesus] spoke to them, "Take courage, it is I; do not be afraid." Peter said to him in reply, "Lord, if it is you, command me to come to you on the water." He said, "Come." Peter got out of the boat and began to walk on the water toward Jesus. But when he saw how [strong] the wind was he became frightened; and, beginning to sink, he cried out, "Lord, save me!" Immediately Jesus stretched out his hand and caught him, and said to him, "O you of little faith, why did you doubt?" After they got into the boat, the wind died down. Those who were in the boat did him homage, saying, "Truly, you are the Son of God."*

Action! It's not so hard to imagine walking on water on a calm day, but would you attempt it when the waves are rolling? Peter did, and he was perfectly fine until he took his eyes off Jesus. Read the passage a second time and notice the thoughts and feelings of the different characters.

Acknowledge: "Come!" Would you have the faith to get out of the boat? When have you felt like you were sinking? Did you call out to Jesus, "Lord, save me!" — or were you silent? Notice your thoughts and feelings that emerge as you meditate with this passage.

Relate: The winds have died down, and the sea is calm. Sit next to Jesus in the boat and talk to him about it.

Receive: Read the passage a third time. How does Jesus respond? What is in Jesus' heart for you?

Respond: Continue the conversation with the one who made you, and who knows you even better than you know yourself. See yourself, and your situation, through Jesus' eyes. Rest in his friendship for a few minutes before moving on.

SUGGESTIONS FOR JOURNALING

1. I feel like I've been rowing all night with the wind and the waves against me when ...
2. I felt like I was sinking when ...
3. Jesus calmed the storm in my heart when ...
4. Sitting in the boat next to Jesus makes me feel ...
5. I ended prayer with a burning desire for ...

_____

_____

_____

_____

_____

_____

_____

_____

_____

_____

_____

_____

_____

_____

_____

_____

_____

_____

_____

After you've journaled, close with a brief conversation thanking God for the experience of his loving presence in today's prayer. Then pray an Our Father.

Thursday of the Third Week in Ordinary Time

SAINTS TIMOTHY AND TITUS, BISHOPS

Saint Timothy was the son of a pagan father and a Hebrew-Christian mother, Eunice (see 2 Tm 1:5). He was a disciple of Saint Paul and accompanied him on his journeys. Paul consecrated him bishop of Ephesus. An early legend says he was killed by a pagan mob when he opposed a pagan festival. Saint Titus was also a friend and disciple of Paul, who ordained him bishop of Crete. Paul wrote three pastoral letters to these two disciples. It is fitting that the day after we celebrate Paul's conversion, we celebrate the feasts of two men whom Paul mentored in the Christian life. Who has mentored you? Whom are you called to mentor?

Preparation: *Come, Holy Spirit, enlighten the eyes of my heart.* Be present to the God who is always present to you. Call to mind his loving care for you and spend the first minute of your prayer just resting in the free, unearned gift of loving and being loved. Let gratitude rise in your heart.

Lectio: Ask for the grace to hear Jesus calling you by name and follow him on the road of daily self-sacrifice. Saint Paul is writing to his young mentee to encourage him in living the Faith and being a good example. Bishop Titus must call his Christian flock to the best possible behavior, for the glory of God and to help evangelize their pagan neighbors. Notice what stirs up inside of you as you read this passage slowly and prayerfully.

TITUS 2:1–14

As for yourself, you must say what is consistent with sound doctrine, namely, that older men should be temperate, dignified, self-controlled, sound in faith, love, and endurance. Similarly, older women should be reverent in their behavior, not slanderers, not addicted to drink, teaching what is good, so that they may train younger women to love their husbands and children, to be self-controlled, chaste, good homemakers, under the control of their husbands, so that the word of God may not be discredited.

Urge the younger men, similarly, to control themselves, showing yourself as a model of good deeds in every respect, with integrity in your teaching, dignity, and sound speech that cannot be criticized, so that the opponent will be put to shame without anything bad to say about us.

Slaves are to be under the control of their masters in all respects, giving them satisfaction, not talking back to them or stealing from them, but exhibiting complete good faith, so as to adorn the doctrine of God our savior in every way.

For the grace of God has appeared, saving all and training us to reject godless ways and worldly desires and to live temperately, justly, and devoutly in this age, as we await the blessed hope, the appearance of the glory of the great God and of our savior Jesus Christ, who gave himself for us to deliver us from all lawlessness and to cleanse for himself a people as his own, eager to do what is good.

Meditatio: What are the godless ways and worldly desires that you see being lived around you? Which of these are also tempting you? Ask the Holy Spirit to convict you where your conduct is unbecoming of a disciple, and to encourage you to persevere in the areas where you are living temperance, justice, and devotion in accord with God's call. Ponder these questions, then read the passage a second time, slowly and prayerfully. Notice what word or phrase speaks to you personally.

Oratio: In the end, no matter how famous or powerful, poor or insignificant we are, we will each answer to Jesus Christ, the just judge. Are you eager to do what is good? What selfish desires or fears get in the way of responding to God's call? Be honest with Jesus about the struggles you might be experiencing. Jesus is just but also merciful. He wants you to do well in the test and is eager to help you accomplish the Father's will for the glory of God. So, ask him for help.

Contemplatio: Read the passage a third time. This time listen for how God answers your prayer. Spend some time with Jesus and his Father before moving on.

SUGGESTIONS FOR JOURNALING

1. The godless ways or worldly desires that most tempt me are ...
2. I struggle with self-control in the area of ...
3. Jesus was with me, and he wanted me to know ...
4. How would my life look different if I strove only to please Jesus and let go of others' expectations and even of my own expectations for myself?
5. I experienced a deeper sense of peace when I realized that ...

After you've journaled, close with a brief conversation thanking God for being with you in today's prayer experience. Then pray an Our Father.

Friday of the Third Week in Ordinary Time

Preparation: *Come, Holy Spirit, enlighten the eyes of my heart.* Be present to the God who is always present to you. Call to mind his loving care for you and spend the first minute of your prayer just resting in the free, unearned gift of loving and being loved. Let gratitude rise in your heart.

Lectio: Ask God for the grace to hear Jesus calling you by name and follow him on the road of the cross. The call to follow Jesus is not fundamentally a call to go somewhere or do something. It is a call to *be with Jesus* and to *learn from him*. We have been learning about Jesus' absolute trust in the Father. Now we realize that Jesus will trust the Father with his life even if it means death, death on the cross. His death means life for the whole world. Paradoxically, every Christian is called to become truly alive through a life of self-sacrifice. Ponder what you are called to as you read this passage today.

MATTHEW 16:21–27

From that time on, Jesus began to show his disciples that he must go to Jerusalem and suffer greatly from the elders, the chief priests, and the scribes, and be killed and on the third day be raised. Then Peter took him aside and began to rebuke him, "God forbid, Lord! No such thing shall ever happen to you." He turned and said to Peter, "Get behind me, Satan! You are an obstacle to me. You are thinking not as God does, but as human beings do."

Then Jesus said to his disciples, "Whoever wishes to come after me must deny himself, take up his cross, and follow me. For whoever wishes to save his life will lose it, but whoever loses his life for my sake will find it. What profit would there be for one to gain the whole world and forfeit his life? Or what can one give in exchange for his life? For the Son of Man will come with his angels in his Father's glory, and then he will repay everyone according to his conduct."

Meditatio: The Anointed One (*Messiah* in Hebrew, *Christos* in Greek) was supposed to be a descendant of King David. He would defeat the enemies of Israel and restore the trampled people to their former glory and rightful place in the world. Just before today's passage, Simon confessed that Jesus was the Messiah. Jesus called him blessed, renamed him "Peter" ("rock"), and promised him the keys to the kingdom of heaven (see Mt 16:13–20). Jesus then makes them promise not to tell anyone and begins to explain that the Messiah will suffer and die a miserable death for the sins of the people. God's ways are not our ways. Sometimes we think that following Jesus will make everything easy and take away all our problems, only to find that life has become harder instead of easier. Instinctively we know that self-sacrifice is the pinnacle of self-giving love. We admire it in others, but we struggle when it is our turn to live self-sacrificing love. Read the passage a second time. Notice how Jesus is calling his disciples to greater faith and to greater love.

Oratio: How is Jesus calling you to a deeper faith in him, and to a deeper love for God and for others? What form does the cross take in your life right now? Speak to Jesus with the same honesty of Peter. Don't be afraid of how Jesus might respond to you.

Contemplatio: Read the passage a third time. Jesus didn't carry his cross alone (see Mt 27:32; Mk 15:21; Lk 23:26). Jesus doesn't expect any Christian to carry his cross alone either. The invitation is to stick with Jesus even when things get difficult. What does Jesus want to say to you? How will Jesus help you? Rest in his loving care for you and his desire that you experience the fullness of life and every good thing.

SUGGESTIONS FOR JOURNALING

1. The person I know who best exemplifies self-sacrificing love is …

2. I laid down my life, picked up my cross, and experienced a deeper sense of meaning and purpose when …
3. Through Jesus' sacrifice on the cross, I have been given the gift of …
4. What worry, fear, hurt, or anxiety is preventing me from living my life as an act of self-giving love?
5. Jesus was with me and wanted me to know …

_____

_____

_____

_____

_____

_____

_____

_____

_____

_____

_____

_____

_____

_____

_____

_____

_____

After you've journaled, close with a brief conversation thanking Jesus for his loving care for you in today's prayer experience. Then pray an Our Father.

Saturday of the Third Week in Ordinary Time

ST. THOMAS AQUINAS, DOCTOR OF THE CHURCH

Born in 1225 to minor Italian nobility, Thomas's family intended for him to become abbot of the prestigious monastery of Monte Cassino in southern Italy. The monks sent him to the University of Naples for his theological studies. There he encountered the Order of Preachers (Dominicans), a new mendicant order that preached the Gospel, lived in poverty, and begged for their food. Against his family's strenuous objections, Thomas left the Benedictines and became a Dominican. He is considered one of the greatest philosophers and theologians of all time. The greatest irony was that his classmates, seeing that he was big and quiet, assumed he was quite stupid and gave him the nickname "The Dumb Ox." Perhaps God's plans for your life do not match up to what your family or classmates see in you.

REVIEW

Preparation: *Come, Holy Spirit, enlighten the eyes of my heart.* Call to mind God's loving care for you and spend the first minute of your prayer just resting in the free, unearned gift of loving and being loved.

This past week, we looked at the call of Jesus' disciples and the call that God has for your life. Review the past week's journal entries. As you do, notice what emerged in the conversation. Here are some questions to help you:

1. Where did I notice God, and what was he doing or saying?
2. How did I respond to what God was doing?
3. I felt God's love most strongly when …
4. I found myself struggling with …
5. I'm grateful for …
6. God seemed to be calling me or inviting me to …
7. This past week, my strongest sense, image, moment, or expe-

rience of God's loving presence was …

Conclude by conversing with God about your week. **Acknowledge** what you have been experiencing. **Relate** it to him. **Receive** what he wants to give you. **Respond** to him. Then savor that image of God's loving presence and rest there for a minute or two. Close with an Our Father.

Week Ten

A Light to the Nations

Welcome to our tenth and final week on our *Oriens* pilgrimage. Our destination is the feast of the Presentation, which commemorates the moment when Mary and Joseph brought baby Jesus to the Temple (see Lk 2:22–40). The law of Moses required the purification of a mother forty days after the birth of a male child (Lv 12:1–8). It also stipulated that the firstborn belonged to the priests. A firstborn cow, sheep, or goat would be sacrificed to God, but not a child. The firstborn son would instead be ransomed by a payment of money (Ex 13:11–16; Nm 18:13–16). This is a reference to the tenth plague in Egypt, the death of the firstborn, and perhaps the sacrifice of Isaac (Gn 22:2–14).

Saint Luke loves the Temple (his Gospel begins and ends in the Temple, and his symbol is the ox, a sacrificial animal). The way he writes about this moment, Jesus isn't being redeemed but rather *presented*. The unseen God has been worshiped here for centuries. Now God himself, in the person of Jesus, is visiting his own Temple. He comes in the humble form of a little baby. However, his visit does not go unseen. Simeon and Anna are symbols of the whole Old Testament. They have grown old waiting for God's promises to be fulfilled. And they have not been disappointed.

Simeon declares: "Now, Master, you may let your servant go / in peace, according to your word, / for my eyes have seen your salvation, / which you prepared in sight of all the peoples, / a light for revelation to the Gentiles, / and glory for your people Israel" (Lk 2:29–32). Remember how, back at the beginning of Advent, we were told to watch? These two old people are still watching. And they are rewarded with a vision of the Savior and Lord whom all the people are waiting for. Simeon and Anna perfectly symbolize what our *Oriens* pilgrimage is all about: faith. God has opened the eyes of their hearts to see God's presence and action in apparently ordinary moments. They recognize Jesus, the light of the world, and they begin to glow with his divine light. My prayer for every pilgrim is that, as you have been watching vigilantly all these weeks, the eyes of your heart have been enlightened by the light of faith. I pray that Christmas time has lit your heart on fire and that you, too, have begun to glow more brightly with God's divine light.

Our prayer pilgrimage journey will end in just a few days. How will you continue your prayer once this book has finished? Flip ahead to page 334 and prayerfully consider some of my suggestions for continuing the journey.

Grace of the Week: On this final week of the journey, we prepare ourselves for Candlemas, the feast of the Presentation. The liturgy that day will invite us, "Let us also, gathered together by the Holy Spirit, proceed to the house of God to encounter Christ. There we shall find him and recognize him in the breaking of the bread, until he comes again, revealed in glory." Ask God for the grace of a burning faith to make our lives worthy of his eternal kingdom.

January 29 — Sunday
Fourth Sunday in Ordinary Time

Preparation: *Come, Holy Spirit, enlighten the eyes of my heart.* Be present to the God who is always present to you. Call to mind his loving care for you and spend the first minute of your prayer just resting in the free, unearned gift of loving and being loved. Let gratitude rise in your heart.

Lectio: Ask God for the grace of a burning faith to make your life worthy of his eternal kingdom. Jesus begins his famous Sermon on the Mount with the Beatitudes. The word in Greek is *makarios,* which means "bless-ed" or "happy." Even today, after two millennia of Christianity, the Gos-pel values are still shockingly countercultural. The world does not in any way cherish poverty, mourning, meekness, those who hunger, those who are merciful, those who are clean of heart, or the peacemakers. Those who live in this way can expect to face persecution. Far from being iron-ic, Jesus is inviting us to realize that these difficult experiences are a greater blessing than winning the lottery or your favorite football team going to the Super Bowl. Read the passage slowly and prayerfully with an open mind and heart.

MATTHEW 5:1–12a (LECTIONARY)
When Jesus saw the crowds, he went up the mountain, and after he had sat down, his disciples came to him. He began to teach them, saying:

> *"Blessed are the poor in spirit,*
> *for theirs is the kingdom of heaven.*
> *Blessed are they who mourn,*
> *for they will be comforted.*
> *Blessed are the meek,*
> *for they will inherit the land.*
> *Blessed are they who hunger and thirst for righteousness,*

> *for they will be satisfied.*
> *Blessed are the merciful,*
>   *for they will be shown mercy.*
> *Blessed are the clean of heart,*
>   *for they will see God.*
> *Blessed are the peacemakers,*
>   *for they will be called children of God.*
> *Blessed are they who are persecuted for the sake of*
>   *righteousness,*
>   *for theirs is the kingdom of heaven.*

> *Blessed are you when they insult you and persecute you*
> *and utter every kind of evil against you falsely because of*
> *me. Rejoice and be glad, for your reward will be great in*
> *heaven."*

Meditatio: Imagine for a moment that the goal of human life is not to amass as much pleasure, power, prestige, or possessions as possible. Rather, human beings were made by love and for love. We are called to a life of self-giving love, which means to *love the Lord our God with all our heart, soul, mind, and strength,* and to *love others as Christ has loved us.* If love is our mission, then the circumstances that help us to truly be ourselves are a blessing. In other words, we are blessed when we are given the opportunity to more deeply love God and neighbor. Do you begin to see what Jesus is getting at? The objectively difficult experiences of our life are invitations to greater love. Ask the Holy Spirit to help you see your life from God's perspective. Read the passage again and notice what speaks to you.

Oratio: Who is it that most perfectly exemplifies these Beatitudes? Look closely and we will see that Jesus himself is poor in spirit (see 2 Cor 8:9); he mourns (Lk 19:41); he is meek (Mt 11:29); he hungers for righteousness (Mt 23:37); he is merciful (Lk 23:34); he is clean of heart (Heb 4:15); he is a peacemaker (Eph 2:14); and he is persecuted. The Beatitudes are like a portrait of Jesus. He is calling you to be like himself. Gaze at the face of Jesus and see his desire to richly bless you. Speak to him from your heart.

Contemplatio: Read the passage a third time. This time receive whatever grace or blessing God desires to give you in this moment. Rest in his love for you with confidence and peace for a few minutes.

SUGGESTIONS FOR JOURNALING

1. The Beatitude that most "looks like Jesus" to me is …
2. The Beatitude that I most struggle to understand is …
3. I most desire the blessing of (pick one of the seven blessings Jesus names) …
4. Jesus is giving me, or inviting me to …
5. Today I will strive to live the Beatitudes more intentionally by …

After you've journaled, close with a brief conversation thanking God for blessing you in today's prayer experience. Then pray an Our Father.

January 30 — Monday

Monday of the Fourth Week in Ordinary Time

Preparation: *Come, Holy Spirit, enlighten the eyes of my heart.* Be present to the God who is always present to you. Call to mind his loving care for you and spend the first minute of your prayer just resting in the free, unearned gift of loving and being loved. Let gratitude rise in your heart.

Lectio: Ask God for the grace of a burning faith so you can share the Good News with others. The Good News is not fundamentally a piece of information but an encounter with a person: Jesus Christ, who loves us and calls us into friendship with himself. The Holy Spirit may, in fact, be calling you to missionary work in neighboring towns or far-off lands. Most of us, however, don't have to go far to find the mission field. Our own children need to hear the Good News (though if they are over a certain age, you might not be the one called to bring it to them). So do the people we meet in our workplace, our social circle, and our local church. Picture yourself "on mission" to a meal at a friend's house, bringing a dish to pass and the Good News along with it. I know this sounds pretty scary. I am not suggesting you *preach* the Gospel; I am suggesting you *bear witness* to Jesus Christ who is himself the Good News. Think about these concepts as you read the Gospel slowly and prayerfully.

MATTHEW 10:1, 5–13, 16–22

Then he summoned his twelve disciples and gave them authority over unclean spirits to drive them out and to cure every disease and every illness. ...

Jesus sent out these twelve after instructing them thus, "Do not go into pagan territory or enter a Samaritan town. Go rather to the lost sheep of the house of Israel. As you go, make this proclamation: 'The kingdom of heaven is at hand.' Cure the sick, raise the dead, cleanse *lepers, drive out demons. Without cost you have received; without cost you are to give. Do not take gold or silver or copper for your belts; no sack for the journey, or a second tunic, or sandals, or walking stick. The laborer deserves his keep. Whatever town or village you enter, look for a worthy person in it, and stay there until you leave. As you enter a house, wish it peace. If the house is worthy, let your peace come upon it; if not, let your peace return to you."* ...

"Behold, I am sending you like sheep in the midst of wolves; so be shrewd as serpents and simple as doves. But beware of people, for they will hand you over to courts and scourge you in their synagogues, and you will be led before governors and kings for my sake as a witness before them and the pagans. When they hand you over, do not worry about how you are to speak or what you are to say. You will be given at that moment what you are to say. For it will not be you who speak but the Spirit of your Father speaking through you. Brother will hand over brother to death, and the father his child; children will rise up against parents and have them put to death. You will be hated by all because of my name, but whoever endures to the end will be saved."

Meditatio: This passage itself might not strike you as Good News. Let's go over the basics. God loves us and he wants a relationship with us. We have all sinned and fallen short of the glory of God. We have forgotten who we are, or perhaps more fundamentally, *whose* we are. We have forgotten that we are God's beloved children and that a relationship with him is the only path to true life. Jesus came to restore us to this relationship by dying for our sins and then calling us to "Come, follow me." You have come to know and to believe in the love God has for us. Should you keep this to yourself? Absolutely not! You are called to *incarnate in your flesh* the love of God. We witness to God's love precisely by being obedient to the Father and by loving others as God has loved us. Our unconditional love is our witness; it will also get us persecuted. How are you being called to unconditional love? Read the passage a second time and let the Holy Spirit speak to you.

Oratio: We cannot give what we have not received. We must first receive God's love if we are able to give it. There are so many, too, whose hearts are closed to love, as yours once was (and perhaps still is, to some extent). Pray for them. Ask the Father to fill you with love until you glow with the warmth and light of his love. Notice some of the people in your life who seem the most closed, cold, or in need of God's love. Pray for them and ask God to fill them with his love too.

Contemplatio: Read the passage a third time. This time listen for how God answers your prayers. He will never leave you or forsake you; he himself is present in you when you are sharing the Good News with others. Rest in his loving presence with you and savor his love for a few minutes before moving on.

SUGGESTIONS FOR JOURNALING

1. Do I see myself as a missionary? Why or why not?
2. What has today's prayer revealed to me about how I am called and to whom I am called to witness?
3. Being a witness to God's love means ...
4. God was with me and wanted to remind me ...
5. What is one concrete way I can maintain my peace in the midst of a crooked and perverse generation (Phil 2:15), or when people refuse to hear or believe the Good News?

_____

_____

_____

_____

_____

_____

_____

_____

_____

_____

_____

_____

_____

_____

_____

_____

_____

_____

After you've journaled, close with a brief conversation thanking God for being with you in today's prayer experience. Then pray an Our Father.

January 31 — Tuesday
Tuesday of the Fourth Week in Ordinary Time

Preparation: *Come, Holy Spirit, enlighten the eyes of my heart.* Be present to the God who is always present to you. Call to mind his loving care for you and spend the first minute of your prayer just resting in the free, unearned gift of loving and being loved. Let gratitude rise in your heart.

Set the Scene: Ask God for the grace of a burning faith and hope in him. Saint James is said to have died in AD 44, which would put his death about a decade after Jesus' death. Remember that Jesus died at Passover, so the early Christians would have been celebrating an early version of Holy Week (Holy Thursday, Good Friday, Easter Sunday) about this same time. Read the passage to set the scene in your mind.

ACTS 12:1–17

About that time King Herod laid hands upon some members of the church to harm them. He had James, the brother of John, killed by the sword, and when he saw that this was pleasing to the Jews he proceeded to arrest Peter also. (It was [the] feast of Unleavened Bread.) He had him taken into custody and put in prison under the guard of four squads of four soldiers each. He intended to bring him before the people after Passover. Peter thus was being kept in prison, but prayer by the church was fervently being made to God on his behalf.

On the very night before Herod was to bring him to trial, Peter, secured by double chains, was sleeping between two soldiers, while outside the door guards kept watch on the prison. Suddenly the angel of the Lord stood by him and a light shone in the cell. He tapped Peter on the side and awakened him, saying, "Get up quickly." The chains fell from his wrists. The angel said to him, "Put on your belt and your sandals." He did so. Then he said to him, "Put on your cloak and follow me." So he followed him out, not realizing that what was happening through the angel was real; he thought he was seeing a vision. They passed the first guard, then the second, and came to the iron gate leading out to the city, which opened for them by itself. They emerged and made their way down an alley, and suddenly the angel left him. Then Peter recovered his senses and said, "Now I know for certain that [the] Lord sent his angel and rescued me from the hand of Herod and from all that the Jewish people had been expecting." When he realized this, he went to the house of Mary, the mother of John who is called Mark, where there were many people gathered in prayer. When he knocked on the gateway door, a maid named Rhoda came to answer it. She was so overjoyed when she recognized Peter's voice that, instead of opening the gate, she ran in and announced that Peter was standing at the gate. They told her, "You are out of your mind," but she insisted that it was so. But they kept saying, "It is his angel." But Peter continued to knock, and when they opened it, they saw him and were astounded. He motioned to them with his hand to be quiet and explained [to them] how the Lord had led him out of the prison, and said, "Report this to James and the brothers." Then he left and went to another place.

Action! Peter will eventually be martyred for his faith in the city of Rome, but today is not his day. The Church is busy praying for him, and God answers their prayers in a way that is at once miraculous and incredibly down-to-earth. Notice the humanity of each character. What is each one thinking or feeling? Read the passage a second time.

Acknowledge: The people were not expecting a miracle and had a hard time accepting it when God granted a miraculous answer to their prayers.

Does your unbelief sometimes stand in the way of the work God wants to do in you and through you? Notice your own thoughts, feelings, and desires in your prayer time today.

Relate: Share your thoughts, feelings, and desires with God.

Receive: Read the passage a third time, or just the part that spoke to you. How does God respond to what you have shared? Can you receive it?

Respond: Continue the conversation with the one who hears your every cry and answers all your prayers in the best way possible. Rest in the communion you have with the Father, the Son, the Holy Spirit, and all the holy ones.

SUGGESTIONS FOR JOURNALING

1. I have a hard time believing that God can, or God will …
2. Through the prayer of the Church, God freed me from …
3. I felt overjoyed when …
4. Through today's prayer, God wants me to know that …
5. I feel called to …

After you've journaled, close with a brief conversation thanking God for the ways he answers you, especially in your prayer time today. Then pray an Our Father.

Wednesday of the Fourth Week in Ordinary Time

Preparation: *Come, Holy Spirit, enlighten the eyes of my heart.* Be present to the God who is always present to you. Call to mind his loving care for you and spend the first minute of your prayer just resting in the free, unearned gift of loving and being loved. Let gratitude rise in your heart.

Set the Scene: Ask God for the grace to be a good steward of the faith, hope, and love you have received. You are probably familiar with a different final judgment from Matthew's Gospel, the one where Jesus says, "Whatever you did for one of these least brothers of mine, you did it for me" (Mt 25:31–46). That passage in Matthew's Gospel functions as a judgment on "the nations," that is, those who do not know Christ. They are judged on how they have treated the Christians. How, then, are Christians judged? Matthew tells us in today's parable. The word *talent* refers to a large weight (different sources say seventy-five to ninety-five pounds). By extension, it also refers to money (similar to how a "pound sterling" was originally a unit of money equivalent to the value of a pound of sterling silver). A silver talent was worth 6,000 days' wages. The point of all these numbers is to help you realize that even the servant with just one talent was still given a lot to work with. Picture one, two, or five large sacks full of coins as you read the passage below.

MATTHEW 25:14–30

[Jesus said, "The kingdom of heaven] will be as when a man who was going on a journey called in his servants and entrusted his possessions to them. To one he gave five talents; to another, two; to a third, one — to each according to his ability. Then he went away. Immediately the one who received five talents went and traded with them, and made another five. Likewise, the one who received two made another two. But the man who received

one went off and dug a hole in the ground and buried his master's money. "After a long time the master of those servants came back and settled accounts with them. The one who had received five talents came forward bringing the additional five. He said, 'Master, you gave me five talents. See, I have made five more.' His master said to him, 'Well done, my good and faithful servant. Since you were faithful in small matters, I will give you great responsibilities. Come, share your master's joy.' Then the one who had received two talents also came forward and said, 'Master, you gave me two talents. See, I have made two more.' His master said to him, 'Well done, my good and faithful servant. Since you were faithful in small matters, I will give you great responsibilities. Come, share your master's joy.' Then the one who had received the one talent came forward and said, 'Master, I knew you were a demanding person, harvesting where you did not plant and gathering where you did not scatter; so out of fear I went off and buried your talent in the ground. Here it is back.' His master said to him in reply, 'You wicked, lazy servant! So you knew that I harvest where I did not plant and gather where I did not scatter? Should you not then have put my money in the bank so that I could have got it back with interest on my return? Now then! Take the talent from him and give it to the one with ten. For to everyone who has, more will be given and he will grow rich; but from the one who has not, even what he has will be taken away. And throw this useless servant into the darkness outside, where there will be wailing and grinding of teeth.'

Action! Not exactly a happy ending. We might be tempted to negotiate: "Exactly how much of a profit do I need to be turning here?" Matthew, the former tax collector, wants Jesus' disciples to see themselves as stewards. We are all recipients of a great treasure that we don't deserve. That treasure is meant to be passed on. As Jesus said yesterday, "Without cost you have received; without cost you are to give" (Mt 10:8). Bishop Robert

Barron is fond of saying that the divine life can only be held "on the fly." If we try to keep God's gifts for ourselves, they quickly fade and vanish. If we give generously, we find that the divine life increases. You are an instrument through which God's love and mercy can flow to others. When we are forgiven, we need to forgive. When we are blessed, we need to share the blessing with others. What blessings have you received? How should you be giving generously? Read the passage a second time.

Acknowledge: What thoughts, feelings, and desires are you experiencing in today's prayer time? What gift has God blessed you with? What is one way that you can be a blessing to others?

Relate: Jesus himself was a good steward of the Father's many gifts. He will show you how. Thank him for his generous blessings. Ask him to show you how to use your blessings for others.

Receive: Read the passage a third time, or just the part that spoke to you. God always has more he wants to give us. When we give away what we have received, we put ourselves in a position to receive even more. God will not be outdone in generosity. What does God want to give you now?

Respond: Receive whatever God is giving you. Respond to his challenge, invitation, or comfort. The greatest gift God has to give is the gift of himself. Spend a few minutes in communion with the Father, Son, and Holy Spirit.

SUGGESTIONS FOR JOURNALING
1. God has blessed me with …
2. I feel challenged, convicted, or encouraged that …
3. I understand stewardship now to mean …
4. One way I am called to be a blessing to others is …
5. I sensed God's presence reminding me …

_____

_____

_____

_____

_____

_____

_____

_____

_____

_____

_____

_____

_____

_____

_____

_____

_____

_____

After you've journaled, close with a brief conversation thanking God, Father, Son, and Holy Spirit for the blessing of this prayer time together. Then pray an Our Father.

February 2 — Thursday
Feast of the Presentation of the Lord

This feast commemorates the Presentation of the Child Jesus in the Temple forty days after his birth in Bethlehem. Traditionally on this day the priest blesses the candles that will be used in church that year. The faithful may also bring candles to be blessed that they will use in their homes. This is the final, formal conclusion to the Nativity of the Lord. The words of Simeon and the procession with candles now point us toward Lent and Easter.

Preparation: *Come, Holy Spirit, enlighten the eyes of my heart.* Be present to the God who is always present to you. Call to mind his loving care for you along your *Oriens* pilgrimage and spend the first minute of your prayer just resting in the free, unearned gift of loving and being loved. Let gratitude rise in your heart.

Set the Scene: The Temple in Jerusalem is the largest and most impressive building most Jews have ever seen; it dominates the Jewish landscape — literally, politically, and religiously. The nation of Israel gathers here to worship the unseen, all-powerful God and to be cleansed of their sins. But there is something greater than the Temple here. God himself is entering his Temple, not with the fanfare of Palm Sunday, but borne in the arms of his virgin mother. Picture the contrast between the awe-inspiring Temple and the humble reality of God's presence. Read the passage slowly and prayerfully.

LUKE 2:22–40 (LECTIONARY)

When the days were completed for their purification
according to the law of Moses,
Mary and Joseph took Jesus up to Jerusalem
to present him to the Lord,
just as it is written in the law of the Lord,

Every male that opens the womb shall be consecrated to
the Lord,
and to offer the sacrifice of
a pair of turtledoves or two young pigeons,
in accordance with the dictate in the law of the Lord.

Now there was a man in Jerusalem whose name was Sim-
eon. This man was righteous and devout,
awaiting the consolation of Israel,
and the Holy Spirit was upon him.
It had been revealed to him by the Holy Spirit
that he should not see death
before he had seen the Christ of the Lord.
He came in the Spirit into the temple;
and when the parents brought in the child Jesus
to perform the custom of the law in regard to him,
he took him into his arms and blessed God, saying:

"Now, Master, you may let your servant go
in peace, according to your word,
for my eyes have seen your salvation,
which you prepared in sight of all the peoples,
a light for revelation to the Gentiles,
and glory for your people Israel."

The child's father and mother were amazed at what was
said about him;
and Simeon blessed them and said to Mary his mother,
"Behold, this child is destined
for the fall and rise of many in Israel,
and to be a sign that will be contradicted
— and you yourself a sword will pierce —
so that the thoughts of many hearts may be revealed."
There was also a prophetess, Anna,
the daughter of Phanuel, of the tribe of Asher.
She was advanced in years,

having lived seven years with her husband after her mar-
riage, and then as a widow until she was eighty-four.
She never left the temple,
but worshiped night and day with fasting and prayer.
And coming forward at that very time,
she gave thanks to God and spoke about the child
to all who were awaiting the redemption of Jerusalem.

When they had fulfilled all the prescriptions
of the law of the Lord,
they returned to Galilee, to their own town of Nazareth.
The child grew and became strong, filled with wisdom;
and the favor of God was upon him.

Action! God's entry into his Temple does not go unnoticed. Simeon and Anna symbolize all the Old Testament patriarchs and matriarchs who trusted in God's promises and waited for the fulfillment of God's plans. Though their eyes have probably grown dim with age, they see more clearly than the rest of the people, because they see with the eyes of their heart — hearts full of faith and love. They are a model for us. Faith allows them to see what others miss and to understand what God is doing even in the humble situations of everyday life. What is going on in the hearts of Simeon and Anna as they gaze at the Christ Child with love and gratitude? Where do you see God the Father and the Holy Spirit? Read the passage again and notice what speaks to you personally.

Acknowledge: How does your heart leap for joy? Ask Mary to let you hold her child. What does it feel like to hold God's Son, and to know that he was born for you, and he will die for you?

Relate: Speak to the Christ Child, heart to heart. Invite him into your heart.

Receive: Open your heart to receive all that God wants to give you.

Respond: Jesus lives in the heart of every believer. Let your heart enter into a deeper communion with his heart. Let him cast out your darkness and fill you with his pure and holy light. Savor his loving presence for a few minutes before moving on.

SUGGESTIONS FOR JOURNALING
1. I was surprised by …
2. The part that most spoke to me was …
3. The greatest gift God has given me on this pilgrimage was …
4. In exchange, I found God wanting me to give him …
5. I ended prayer wanting …

After you've journaled, close with a brief conversation giving thanks to God for his humble, loving presence. Then pray an Our Father.

The Presentation of the Lord (Candlemas)

AT THE MASS

The people gather in the chapel or other suitable place outside the church where the Mass will be celebrated. They carry unlighted candles. The priest and his ministers wear white vestments. While the candles are being lighted, this canticle may be sung: *The Lord will come with mighty power, and give light to the eyes of all who serve him, alleluia.* Then the priest introduces the Mass:

Dear brothers and sisters, forty days have passed since we celebrated the joyful feast of the Nativity of the Lord. Today is the blessed day when Jesus was presented in the Temple by Mary and Joseph. Outwardly he was fulfilling the Law, but in reality he was coming to meet his believing people. Prompted by the Holy Spirit, Simeon and Anna came to the Temple. Enlightened by the same Spirit, they recognized the Lord and confessed him with exultation. So let us also, gathered together by the Holy Spirit, proceed to the house of God to encounter Christ. There we shall find him and recognize him in the breaking of the bread, until he comes again, revealed in glory.

Then he blesses the candles:

Let us pray. O God, source and origin of all light, who on this day showed to the just man Simeon the Light for revelation to the Gentiles, we humbly ask that, in answer to your people's prayers, you may be pleased to sanctify with your blessing ✠ these candles, which we are eager to carry in praise of your name, so that, treading the path of virtue, we may reach that light which never fails. Through Christ our Lord.

R: Amen.

Let us go forth in peace.

R: In the name of Christ. Amen.

Once a Pilgrim, Always a Pilgrim

Pilgrimages always seem to end abruptly. You strive to reach your destination, you struggle on the road, it seems as though you'll never get there. Then you realize it's the final day, the final miles, and the place of pilgrimage is just over the next hill! You have made it to your destination. You bask in the feeling of success, promise to stay in touch with your fellow pilgrims, and struggle to explain to your family what has happened to you.

Then it is back to your old life. But the old life looks different now; the journey has changed you. You see yourself, God, and the world around you in a different light. Hopefully you, too, have become a light. Christmas time has lit your heart with the warmth and light of God's love. Keep tending your candle! Keep burning and glowing with the light of faith. Carry that light to the dark corners of the world so that the light of God's love will spread to every heart and home.

REVIEW OF REVIEWS

When you have a little time, flip back to the very first day of your pilgrimage, Sunday, November 27, and look at how it all began. Then take a journey through the eight Saturday and one Friday review day (pages 45, 78, 104, 142, 174, 209, 238, 269, and 301). Notice what was coming up. Reflect on where you have been and how God has been with you on the journey. Notice how the journey has changed you.

SUGGESTIONS FOR JOURNALING
1. How did God meet me on the road?
2. There's so much! But the part that most spoke to me was …
3. God was telling me that …
4. I was able to let go of …
5. The deepest desire that has emerged in my heart was …
6. The greatest gift God has given me on this pilgrimage is …
7. In exchange, I found God asked that I would give him the

gift of …

8. If I was going to try to put into words my newfound relationship with God, I would describe it as …

_____

_____

_____

_____

_____

_____

_____

_____

_____

_____

_____

_____

_____

_____

_____

_____

_____

_____

_____

_____

_____

_____

Acknowledge what the pilgrimage meant to you. **Relate** it to God. **Receive** what he wants to give you. **Respond** to him. Then savor God's loving presence and rest there for a minute or two. Close with an Our Father.

The Journey Continues

I always tell pilgrims that they need to keep walking. Our journey is never done until we *come to the end of our pilgrimage and enter the presence of God.*[*] Here are some suggestions for you to continue the journey:

- Buy a journal. At the end of each day, answer two questions: 1) Where did I see God today? 2) What was God doing? Use the ARRR prayer form to pray with your daily experiences and journal the fruits of your prayer (p. 275).
- On the following pages, I give you outlines for four different forms of prayer. You might even want to tear out those pages and keep them with your journal.
- Start praying with the daily Scripture readings. You can find each day's readings at usccb.org/bible/readings/. Depending on the reading, you can use *lectio divina* or imaginative prayer for your prayer each day (see the Prayer Outlines, pp. 339 and 341).
- Subscribe to a monthly missal. I have used Magnificat for years, and I find it very helpful. It includes prayer for morning and evening, the daily readings, and some reflections and additional prayers. There are many other monthly missals to choose from, and all of them will help you pray daily.
- Need more help journaling? Check out the Monk Manual at monkmanual.com. This resource provides reflection space and prompts for you on a daily, weekly, and monthly basis. It helps you live life with more reflection and purpose.
- Another great journal option is Every Sacred Sunday, which has readings and journal space for Sundays and holy days. Check it out at https://everysacredsunday.com.

---

*Antiphon 1, Monday Week II, Morning Prayer, The English translation of the Liturgy of the Hours (Four Volumes) © 1974, International Commission on English in the Liturgy Corporation.

- Subscribe to my homily podcast. Learn more at PilgrimPriest.us/podcast.
- OSV has a number of Bible study resources. Browse their offerings at www.osvcatholicbookstore.com/product-category/bibles-bible-studies. Consider not only participating in a Bible study, but actually leading one at your local church or in your home.
- Lent is coming up soon. Start reflecting and praying about a theme for Lent and how to live Lent more intentionally.
- Consider making a real, honest-to-goodness walking pilgrimage. My diocese hosts the Walk to Mary every year, a one-day walking pilgrimage. Learn more at walktomary.com. Check out my website for the article "A Step-by-Step Guide to Walking Pilgrimages."

PRAYER
OUTLINES

LECTIO DIVINA

Lectio divina can be used with any passage from Scripture. T.
use Scripture as a conversation starter for a deep, personal co.
with the God who inspired it. Don't rush each step; let them .
unfold. Remember that the goal is spending quality time with t.
who loves you. As you read, think, talk, and listen, you will learn to
time with God like an old friend.

Preparation: *Come, Holy Spirit, enlighten the eyes of my heart.* Be present
to the God who is always present to you. Call to mind his loving care
for you and spend the first minute of your prayer just resting in the free,
unearned gift of loving and being loved. Let gratitude rise in your heart.

Lectio: Ask God for whatever grace it is you desire to receive in today's
prayer time. Read the passage through, slowly and prayerfully.

Meditatio: Read the passage again. Turn it over in your mind. The ancients
compared meditation to a cow chewing its cud. What was the cultural context? What did the author mean? Perhaps a particular word, phrase, or
idea speaks to us. Perhaps it connects to a previous meditation or another
Scripture passage. What are your feelings as you read the passage?

Oratio: Prayer must be a conversation between persons. Turn to God
and begin a conversation with him. Speak to him what is on your heart
— your thoughts, feelings, fears, and desires.

Contemplatio: Read the passage a third time. Now just receive what is
on God's heart — his thoughts, feelings, and desires. Spend some time
receiving God's love and resting in it. Prayer is experiencing how our Father looks at us with love. Holiness is learning to live in his long, loving
gaze every moment of our life.

SUGGESTIONS FOR JOURNALING

Journaling isn't an essential part of the prayer, but I find it helps me to deepen the experience when I put into words what was happening in my prayer time. You might find questions like these helpful, or you might make your own list of journal questions.

1. The part that most spoke to me was …
2. What I brought to the Lord was …
3. God gave me …
4. I received a new insight, understanding, or sense of myself …
5. Apply something from the passage to your own life. (For example, a passage about John the Baptist: Who pointed out Jesus to me? When did I point out Jesus to another person? What virtue of John the Baptist do I feel called to imitate?)

After you've journaled, close with a brief conversation giving thanks to God for the prayer time together. End with an Our Father or another favorite prayer.

IMAGINATIVE PRAYER

Imaginative prayer helps us disconnect from this present moment to connect us with the deep reality of God's loving, invisible presence with us right now. The goal is not to build imaginary castles in the air, but to look into the Bible and, through it, encounter the God who was present in the moment when the biblical passage was written and is present here with you today. The imagination helps to break the ice and start the conversation as you spend quality time with God. It works best with Scriptures that have a lot of visual description or action to them.

Preparation: *Come, Holy Spirit, enlighten the eyes of my heart.* Be present to the God who is always present to you. Call to mind his loving care for you and spend the first minute of your prayer just resting in the free, unearned gift of loving and being loved. Let gratitude rise in your heart.

Set the Scene: Ask God for whatever grace it is you desire to receive in today's prayer time. Read the passage through and picture the scene in your mind. Choose the time of day and the scenery. Populate it with people dressed in period clothes. (Alternatively, you can picture the scene happening in your own city or neighborhood.)

Action! Read the passage a second time and play the scene forward in your mind. Notice how the participants react and what they are thinking and feeling. Notice where Jesus is and what he is doing. (You can also notice Mary, God the Father, the Holy Spirit, etc.). Place yourself in the scene.

Acknowledge: Read the passage a third time. What does this passage stir up in your mind and heart? Pay attention to your thoughts, feelings, and desires. Don't worry whether they are "correct," just notice them without any judgment.

Relate: As the scene is finished, spend some time in conversation with Jesus. You can walk with him, sit with him in the scene, or just be aware of his presence in your prayer space. Share your thoughts, feelings, desires, and fears, honestly and openly.

Receive: How does God respond to what you have shared? What is in God's heart for you? Receiving isn't meant to be hard work. It is about relaxing into God's loving presence, focusing on him, and noticing what word, Scripture passage, feeling, or reminder might come.

Respond: This is a chance to deepen the conversation. Ask a question about what God seems to be saying, or just say, "Thank you." And like good friends, let yourself just enjoy God's company for a little while.

SUGGESTIONS FOR JOURNALING

1. Something in my life that connected with the story ...
2. As the scene played out, what struck me was ...
3. I talked to Jesus about ...
4. I sensed he wanted me to know, or to give me, or remind me ...
5. I left prayer with a new insight, understanding, or a call to a new way of thinking or acting ...

After you've journaled, close with a brief conversation giving thanks to God for your prayer experience. Then pray an Our Father or another favorite prayer.

Relational Prayer (ARRR)

Relational prayer is a great way of praying with the experiences of every-day life. No matter what kinds of struggles or challenges you are facing, you can always pause and take a moment to give them to God. Here's how you do it:

Preparation: *Come, Holy Spirit, enlighten the eyes of my heart.* Be present to the God who is always present to you. Call to mind his loving care for you and spend the first minute of your prayer just resting in the free, unearned gift of loving and being loved. Let gratitude rise in your heart.

Acknowledge: Notice what is going on inside of you — your thoughts, feelings, and desires. If you are examining a recent event, try to fill in the blank, such as: "When that person did/said/acted that way, it made me feel ____." There may be a number of different feelings that happened in quick succession. If your feelings are so strong they're making it hard to concentrate, pray the name of Jesus a few times and stick with the preparation period until you notice his peaceful presence. When the feeling is anger, try to notice what you were thinking and feeling just before you got angry. That can be a clue to where the anger came from and what God might want you to share with him. If you are feeling numb, or have no feelings at all, ask the Holy Spirit to help you connect with your feelings. We may need to give ourselves permission to feel our feelings.

Relate: Share with the Lord what is going on inside of you. Be honest with God. Sometimes we are mad at God himself because he appears to be ruining our lives or ignoring our prayers. You can get mad at God. Tell him how you feel, even if it includes inappropriate words. It's really important that we be completely honest. Do not try to ask God to give you something or do something at this stage. Just tell him what is going on with you.

Receive: Now we shift our attention from us and our problems to God. This is where I often got stuck when I was learning this prayer form.

Picture this scene: I'm struggling with something. A good friend comes and stands next to me. I point out the problem, tell him everything, and he listens patiently. God and I are looking at my problem together. Now, I turn to focus on my friend. What is in his heart for me? How does he look at me? It's his turn to talk. Sometimes it's just knowing that he cares, a feeling of peace, or that I am not alone in my problem. Sometimes it might be a Scripture passage or a few words to put me in my place or add perspective. Like with any good friend, it may not be exactly what I want to hear, but it will be what I need to hear.

Respond: If what he just gave you is hard to receive, tell him so. If it comforts you, thank him. Even if you don't get anything at this time, you can be confident that God will answer you when he is ready and will give you what you really need. So, keep your eyes and ears open in case he has more to say or give you later.

Sharing your burdens with God makes them melt like snow in the sunshine. It's almost like magic, but better. We call it "grace." Practice this prayer time with the experiences of your everyday life.

SUGGESTIONS FOR JOURNALING

1. My strongest thought, feeling, or emotion was …
2. I needed to share with God that …
3. God wanted me to know …
4. In the course of my prayer time, I realized that …
5. I ended prayer with a new way of thinking, acting, responding, or believing …
6. I feel called by God to …

Feel free to journal whatever from the above struck you. Then spend a few minutes thanking God for the quality time together, and end with an Our Father or another favorite prayer.

The Saturday Review

I like to keep an old canning jar as a "Gratitude Jar." I start at New Year's, and each Saturday I write on a slip of paper the one thing I am most grateful for that week and add it to the jar. At the end of the year, I dump out the jar and review my blessings. If you're interested in adopting this practice for yourself, a Saturday review like those we did throughout the *Oriens* pilgrimage can help fill your jar.

Preparation: *Come, Holy Spirit, enlighten the eyes of my heart.* Call to mind his loving care for you and spend the first minute of your prayer just resting in the free, unearned gift of loving and being loved. Let gratitude rise in your heart.

Flip back through your past week's journal entries. If you don't journal, cast your mind back through your week. Where did you go to Mass last Sunday? What did you receive from Mass? What was a high point this week? What was a low point? Here are some questions to help you:

1. My biggest blessing in the past week was …
2. My biggest challenge was …
3. Where did I notice God, and what was he doing or saying?
4. How did I respond to what God was doing?
5. I felt God's love most strongly when …
6. I'm grateful for …
7. This past week, my strongest sense, image, moment, or experience of God's loving presence was …

Journal for a little while whatever you are experiencing.

Conclude by conversing with God about your week. **Acknowledge** what you have been experiencing. **Relate** it to him. **Receive** what he wants to give you. **Respond** to him. Then savor that image of God's loving presence and rest there for a minute or two. Close with a Glory Be.

Acknowledgments

Thank you to Our Lady, the Queen of Heaven, who appeared in Champion, Wisconsin, in 1859. Thank you to the Shrine of Our Lady of Good Help for welcoming pilgrims as a place of prayer, peace, and hospitality.

I am grateful to Tim, my first partner on pilgrimage, and all my fellow walking pilgrims through the years. Your companionship has richly blessed and encouraged me.

To Father Paul, Father Tom, Father Ryan, Father Michael and my priestly fraternity group, Father Looney, and the priests and people of the Diocese of Green Bay.

Thank you to the good people of Saint John the Evangelist, Ss. Mary and Hyacinth, Saint Wenceslaus, and Ss. James and Stanislaus Parish.

Thank you to the Institute for Priestly Formation for my training as a spiritual director. This book is a fruit of their ministry, which is why I am donating my royalties to support their work. Learn more at www.priestlyformation.org.

Thank you to my loving family, and especially my parents Jim and Marion, who often tell me they love me and are proud of me.

To Tracy Stewart and Mary Beth Giltner of Our Sunday Visitor for helping shape this third (and best) edition of *Oriens*.

And to you, my fellow *Oriens* pilgrim. I wrote this book for you. I hope we meet some day, in this life or the next. The best is yet to come!

About the Author

Father Joel Sember was ordained a priest in 2007 for the Diocese of Green Bay, Wisconsin. He has extensive experience as a parish priest and two years of service in campus ministry. He made a thirty-day Ignatian silent retreat and later completed the Spiritual Direction Training Program through the Institute for Priestly Formation in Omaha, Nebraska. He holds a BA in philosophy and Catholic studies from the University of St. Thomas, a bachelor's in sacred theology from the Pontifical Gregorian University, and a license in sacred theology from the Pontifical University Santa Croce in Rome. He has completed a dozen walking pilgrimages. He currently serves as pastor of four parishes in rural northeastern Wisconsin. Between ministry and parish meetings, he rides a motorcycle and paddles a kayak around great Wisconsin lakes. You can listen to his homily podcast every Sunday at PilgrimPriest.us.

About the Artist

Lisa Dorschner is an artist from Wisconsin inspired through prayer, dedication to God, and the ongoing invitation to draw closer to Jesus through faith amidst life's challenges and in gratitude for many blessings. As a full-time art teacher, she encourages her students to seek beauty in the world and share their artwork with others. Lisa is a mother of four, and enjoys being an extraordinary minister of holy Communion, lector, and healing prayer minister for her parish in Oshkosh, Wisconsin.

About the Cover Art

Return to Me by Lisa Dorschner

We often think of a pilgrimage as a journey to a distant destination. A pilgrimage, however, is also a journey of the heart. Part shepherd, part pilgrim, the figure in the foreground is already anticipating Christmas by the color of his clothing. His shoulder bag sports a seashell, the traditional symbol of pilgrimages to the Holy Land and to Compostela. The road ahead promises suffering (the signpost shaped like a cross) but also new life symbolized by the shoot sprouting from the stump of Jesse and a rose ere blooming despite the cold weather. The road is not completely visible; what surprises await him? The eight-pointed star points to a destination both earthly and heavenly as the "dawn from on high" begins to break on the horizon. Though the destination feels distant, there is something homey and familiar about it. Have we been there before? You must walk the road yourself to ponder that mystery.